AF316782

THROUGH MY EYES: UNVEILING THE TRUTH OF THE HEART

SASHA DIXON

"If even one poem in this collection touched your heart, made you feel seen, or helped you through something your review could help someone else find that same moment of connection. Just a few words mean the world."

Copyright © 2025 Sasha Dixon All rights reserved.

Library of Congress Control Number: 2026912918

ISBN: 979-8-2340-78315

DEDICATION

I dedicate this book to Jesus. Had it not been for Him, I would not have made it through my trials. I have felt every emotion, but through it all, His presence has been my strength.

I also want to thank every person I have crossed paths within this journey my friends, family, and partners of you have played a vital role in my growth and evolution, teaching me invaluable lessons along the way.

When I was eight years old, I was adopted by my grandparents, Dorthy Allen and Harvey Lee Allen. Being raised by them two people who have shared 45 years of marriage, has given me a lifetime of wisdom to carry with me. Their love, guidance, and unwavering support have shaped the person I am today.

Table of Contents

Love and Relationships

TEAMWORK ACKNOWLEDGMENT

I want to extend my deepest gratitude to Skyler Warren, my friend, collaborator, and creative partner. Skyler and I first met as classmates in the Myers School of Art at The University of Akron, and from the very beginning, we shared a natural rhythm when it came to creating art together.

Over the years, Skyler has been the visionary behind every one of my book covers, turning concepts into stunning visuals that bring my stories to life. One of the most memorable moments in our creative journey was when I shared a dream of seeing my daughter, Bella Lee, brought to life as a cartoon for a children's book. Skyler captured that vision perfectly, transforming it into something magical.

Whenever I come to him with an idea, no matter how big or small, he meets me with excitement, dedication, and extraordinary talent. Together, we've built more than just covers; we've built a legacy of creativity and collaboration.
Thank you, Skyler, for always showing up, for believing in my visions, and for bringing them to reality with heart, soul, and brilliance. Here's to many more creations together.

ACKNOWLEDGMENTS

I would like to take a moment to acknowledge and thank Jesus Christ for His unwavering presence in my life, guiding me through every moment of pain and triumph. His love and grace have been the anchor in my stormy times.

I also want to express my deepest gratitude to my friends and family. Your support, understanding, and encouragement have been invaluable in helping me pull through these hard times. I am blessed to have such a strong, loving circle around me. Thank you for walking with me on this journey of self-discovery, healing, and growth.

"The Weight of a Fan"

I spoke of a fan, just a breeze in the air,
A whisper of comfort to carry me there
To classrooms and crayons, to laughter and light,
A new little chapter, both hopeful and bright.

Your brow drew a furrow, your jaw took a line,
As if I had borrowed what once had been mine.
A simple possession, yet something had stirred,
In silence, your body had shouted a word.

It wasn't the fan or the dollars it cost,
But maybe the fear of what else might be lost.
Of mornings not shared or routines that would shift,
Of moments now caught in an invisible rift.

Perhaps it was pride, or control held too tight,
Or shadows of feelings that woke in the night.
A job that I wanted, a move toward the sun
But change has its price, even when it seems fun.

A daughter, a dream, and a doorway ahead
Yet something unspoken was quietly said.
Your silence, a mirror, reflecting the pain
Of things we don't mention but feel all the same.

So, let's talk, not of fans, but of fears that remain,
Of joy and of worry, of love's growing strain.
For even small gestures can pull at the seams,
When stitched to the fabric of long-hidden dreams.

Proverbs 20:5 (KJV)

*"Counsel in the heart of
man is like deep water; but a man of understanding will draw it out."*

"The Mirror Isn't Broken"

If you love bullies, wounds with control,
They're dimming your light to darken your soul.
It isn't just yelling or cruel verbal rain
It's silence, manipulation, and shame.

They criticize daily, chip at your pride,
Make rules on who's near you, then stand to the side.
With threats or with guilt, they get their own way,
While you lose a little more peace every day.

They mock and belittle, they laugh when you cry,
They twist up the truth and then question your mind.
They say that you're "crazy," deny what they've done,
Gaslight your memory, until you feel none.

It's not your fault, not even a bit.
Love doesn't come dressed in control or in grit.
It grows in respect, in a warm, open space
Not fear, not confusion, not walking on lace.

You're strong to speak out, and brave to be here,
In a world that can shrink when you're ruled by fear.
You're not imagining all you have seen,
Their truth isn't truth if it's cruel and mean.

Sometimes it's their trauma, their pain left unchecked,
But pain's not a reason to harm or neglect.
Insecurities taught them to lie or deceive
But none of those reasons give cause to mistreat.

They learned to deflect when they couldn't be wrong,
To rewrite the script and silence your song.
But their wounds are theirs you're not their repair,
You're not here to bleed just to show them you care.

You matter. You're worthy. Your voice should be heard.
You shouldn't be doubting each memory, each word.
You're not overthinking. You're not too "sensitive."

You're someone who simply deserves to know how to live.

So how long has this cycle been taking its toll?
And how does it feel when they chip at your soul?
I'm here when you're ready your story is yours.
You don't have to walk through this pain anymore.

Psalm 34:18 (KJV)
"The Lord is nigh unto them that are of a broken heart; and saveth such as be of a contrite spirit."

"Control and Entitlement"

You say it's love, but bends your will,
As if your silence makes you still.
you speak of futures etched in stone,
Yet builds them all without your tone.

You cast your no as mere delay,
A pause before you "see your way."
But choice is not a waiting game
Your voice should never spark their shame.

A role you write, without your pen,
You see your mother not if, but when.
As though your heart's a means to end,
Not sovereign self, but one who bends.

You cloak you're want in flattery's glow,
Then weaves in guilt so soft and slow.
Through holy words, you cast your net,
But faiths are not forged from silent debt.

Your mother's dreams, your culture's chain,
You wear them not with pride, but pain.
And so, you lay that weight on you,
As if your dreams aren't worthy too.

You speak of sons, of names to keep,
But lineage is not love that's deep.
A legacy that costs your voice
It was never built on mutual choice.

Your fears that no means you might leave,
That without kids, you might deceive.
You need a child to feel complete
But wholeness doesn't start with need.

You want the picture, not the truth,
A life designed in shallow youth.
With checklist dreams and fantasy,

You won't hear no it breaks your spell,

You dodge where the hard truths dwell.
Emotionally, you hide from light,
Mistakes persistence for what's right.

But this is more than motherhood
It's your own soul misunderstood.
Your faith, your body, your command
They're not for them to take or plan.

If love means power, tilted scales,
Where pressure speaks and silence pales,
Then call it what it truly is:
Control disguised as future bliss.

So let your "no" be firm and clear,
For love that's real won't trade on fear.
And should he balk, then let him go
You are not his shape or own.

Let choice be love, and love be choice,
In every tear, in every voice.

Galatians 5:1 (KJV)

"Stand fast therefore in the liberty wherewith Christ hath made us free and be not entangled again with the yoke of bondage."

"Loved As I Am"

They chase a dream, not flesh and bone,
A version of life that's not their own.
They see in you a perfect frame,
But miss the soul, they miss your name.

They want the role, the image clear,
A partner shaped by pride or fear.
Not for your laugh, or how you cry
But how you fit the box they try.

And yet you twist, and bend, and bleed,
To meet a hunger, they don't need.
You wear a mask, suppress your light,
To make their heavy wrong feel right.

But love should never ask you to
Shrink down to half of what is true.
You're not a puzzle piece to shove
Into a life that mimics love.

It hurts, I know it tears your core,
To give and still be asked for more.
To feel like worth is just a test,
To be enough, but not the best.

You're not a perfect project,
Or proof of someone's self-respect.
You're not a mirror for their dream,
You're real, you breathe, you cry, you scream.

Support would look like hands held tight,
A soul that sees you in the night.
No fixing, pushing, pressure games
Just someone soft who speaks your name.

Someone who listens, doesn't mold,
Who loves you fiercely, who loves you bold.
Not for the future you might be,

But every thread of you they see.

So, ask for less? No, ask for more.
Ask for the kind who won't ignore.
Because you are worthy, deep and true,
Of love that simply chooses you.

Romans 8:38–39 (KJV)

"For I am persuaded, that neither death, nor life, nor angels, nor principalities, nor powers, nor things present, nor things to come,
Nor height, nor depth, nor any other creature, shall be able to separate us from the love of God, which is in Christ Jesus our Lord."

"My Voice, My Faith, My Fight"

I said it clearly: I don't want more,
Yet they keep knocking on that door.
A choice that's mine, not theirs to make,
But still they push, and hearts will break
.

A mother speaks, he nods along,
As if my "no" was said all wrong.
Like I'm a vessel, not a soul,
Like motherhood's my only goal.

Entitled hands reach for my peace,
Control disguised as love's deceit.
They frame my faith in their own mold,
But mine is quiet, fierce, and bold.

They say they walk this path with grace,
Yet pressure paints a different face.
When faith's a chain and not a light,
Then even prayer can feel like fight.

He hears my words, but not my cry,
Just waits me out, lets minutes fly.
Like time will turn my "no" to "yes,"
While I sit drowning in this mess.

This isn't love, it's something less
A game of power, masked finesse.
If love won't listen, won't align,
Then whose heart is truly mine?

My womb is not a battleground,
For silence screamed and truths unbound.
My future's not a gift to take,
My spirit's not for them to break.

Respect means hearing what I feel,
Not framing pain as some ideal.
And faith should never be a chain
That binds me tighter to their reign.

So here I stand, alone but proud,
With voice unshaken, firm, and loud.
I owe no child, I owe no role
I only owe truth to my soul.

2 Timothy 1:7 (KJV)

"For God hath not given us the spirit of fear; but of power, and of love, and of a sound mind."

"Envy"
(A Poetic Exploration of the Shadow Within)

You walk with grace, they watch your stride,
Yet loathe the way you glow inside.
They mimic moves, they steal your shade,
But in their chest, a storm is laid.

For envy seeds a twisted tree,
Its roots in dark identity.
They want your light, your voice, your flair,
But curse the fact it isn't theirs.

Your presence whispers all they lack,
So, love and hate dance back-to-back.
They wear your smile, then scorn your name,
Admire the fire but damn the flame.

Within their soul, a mirror cracked,
Reflects the self they think they lack.
They copy close to feel complete,
But shrink with shame at your heartbeat.

Their shadow stirs Jung's silent scream,
Projecting ghosts from broken dreams.
What they condemn, they can't admit:
That deep inside, your traits would fit.

Conflicted hearts, a tangled wire,
Were adoration fights with ire.
To want, to hate, to push, to pull
It's how the fractured mind gets full.

Sometimes obsession takes the wheel,
And narcissism seals the deal.
A game of masks, a grand charade,
Where envy sharpens every blade.

But no, dear soul, it isn't you
It's wounds in them, long overdue.

Your light reveals what they conceal,
Pain too raw, a truth too real.

So set your boundaries firm and kind,
Protect your peace, expand your mind.
And understand: their stormy sea
It is not your fault, nor destiny.

They wear your skin, yet cannot be
The soul that walks so openly.
And though their eyes may burn with spite,
Your shadow stands in honest light.

James 3:16 (KJV):

"For where envying and strife is, there is confusion and every evil work."

"The Mirror You Hate to See"

I am who you pretend to be,
The bold, the bright, the wild, the free.
With style and charm, I walk with grace,
Success and love sit in my space.

You watch me close, yet turn away,
But every step, you still replay.
You chase a gap you cannot close,
A garden blooms while yours just grows.

You copy me, but not for flair,
You're searching for yourself there.
You mimic moves, adopt my tone,
Yet feel more lost, more not your own.

Your hatred is a veiled disguise,
For fear and fire behind your eyes.
It's not disliked its envy's sting,
That makes you curse while worshipping.

A storm of love and spite you brew,
You hate me yet you want me too.
Your gaze is sharp, yet locked on mine,
A twisted dance in tangled lines.

You follow me in thought and dress,
But all it brings is more distress.
This needs to win, to one up me,
Reflects your deep identity.

Your game is cruel, your mask is tight,
Yet still you lurk just out of sight.
Obsessed, possessed by what you lack,
You wear my shadow on your back.

But know this truth that cuts like flame:
To be yourself is not a game.
No need to steal what you could grow,
No need to dim my light to glow.
So, face the mirror look inside.

No more to run from, none to hide.
The peace you seek won't come from me
It lives within, if you break free.

Galatians 6:4 (KJV):

"But let every man prove his own work, and then shall he have rejoicing in himself alone, and not in another."

"The Rhythm of Real"

In the hush of hearts where silence grows,
A whisper weaves what no one knows.
We trade our truths for sweet disguise,
And bury hope in tired lies.

You said you'd come, you said you'd care,
But it left me waiting, empty air.
A promise made, a ghostly song
It echoes loud but feels so wrong.

I danced alone in rooms of need,
While feeding love on shallow feed.
Each "yes" you gave a thread gone slack,
A forward step, then turning back.

Is love a vow, or just pretense?
A borrowed warmth, or deep incense?
The things we do, not what we say,
Are what the soul recalls each day.

But still I wait, with hopeful eyes,
A fool beneath forgiving skies.
Yet even fools can wake from dreams,
And see the cracks in golden beams.

So, hold me not with idle breath,
But build with hands, or love to death.
For rhythm lies in truth revealed
The heart, once broken, must be healed.

1 John 3:18 (KJV)

"My little children, let us not love in word, neither in tongue; but indeed and in truth."

"The Smile That Hurt"

I'm sorry you're in pain
It's more than mouth; it's more than strain.
It cuts beneath the skin and bone,
A kind of ache makes you feel alone.

A gentle touch, a tender sore,
You braced yourself, then felt some more
Your son bumped in, a quick surprise,
But what came next broke softer ties.

He smiled. You flinched. You searched his face
Not love, not warmth, not safe embrace.
But something cold behind the grin,
A subtle joy beneath the skin.

When we are hurt, we seek a hand,
A kind word we can understand.
But laughter where you hoped for grace
can feel like knives in softest place.

The body knows what minds might miss
It reads a smirk, mistrusts a kiss.
It guards the heart, it sounds alarms
When smiles conceal emotional harms.

Perhaps resentment hides in jest,
A shadowed grudge that's unconfessed.
Or power plays that make one feel
Superior when you must heal.

Or maybe he just doesn't see
The ways that empathy should be.
He masks discomfort with a joke,
But leaves your trust in wisps of smoke.

Whatever cause, your gut is wise
It senses truth behind the eyes.
If you felt mocked, not met with care,

Then something real is broken there.

And pain is pain it's not a game,
No glance or giggle should inflame.
Your wound was fresh, your heart was raw,
You needed love not what you saw.

So, take this moment, hold it tight,
Your instincts sparked for reasons right.
This may be one time or a thread
A pattern spun where love has bled.

Your voice is strong, your truth is clear,
You're not too soft, you're right to fear.
You deserve kindness, not charades,
Not warmth that dims or slowly fades.

So now reflect, decide what's real
What do you need to truly heal?
Is this a blip, or deeper pain?
A passing cloud, or steady rain?

Whatever path you choose to chart,
Begin by listening to your heart.
You're not too much, you're not insane
You're just a soul who spoke their pain.

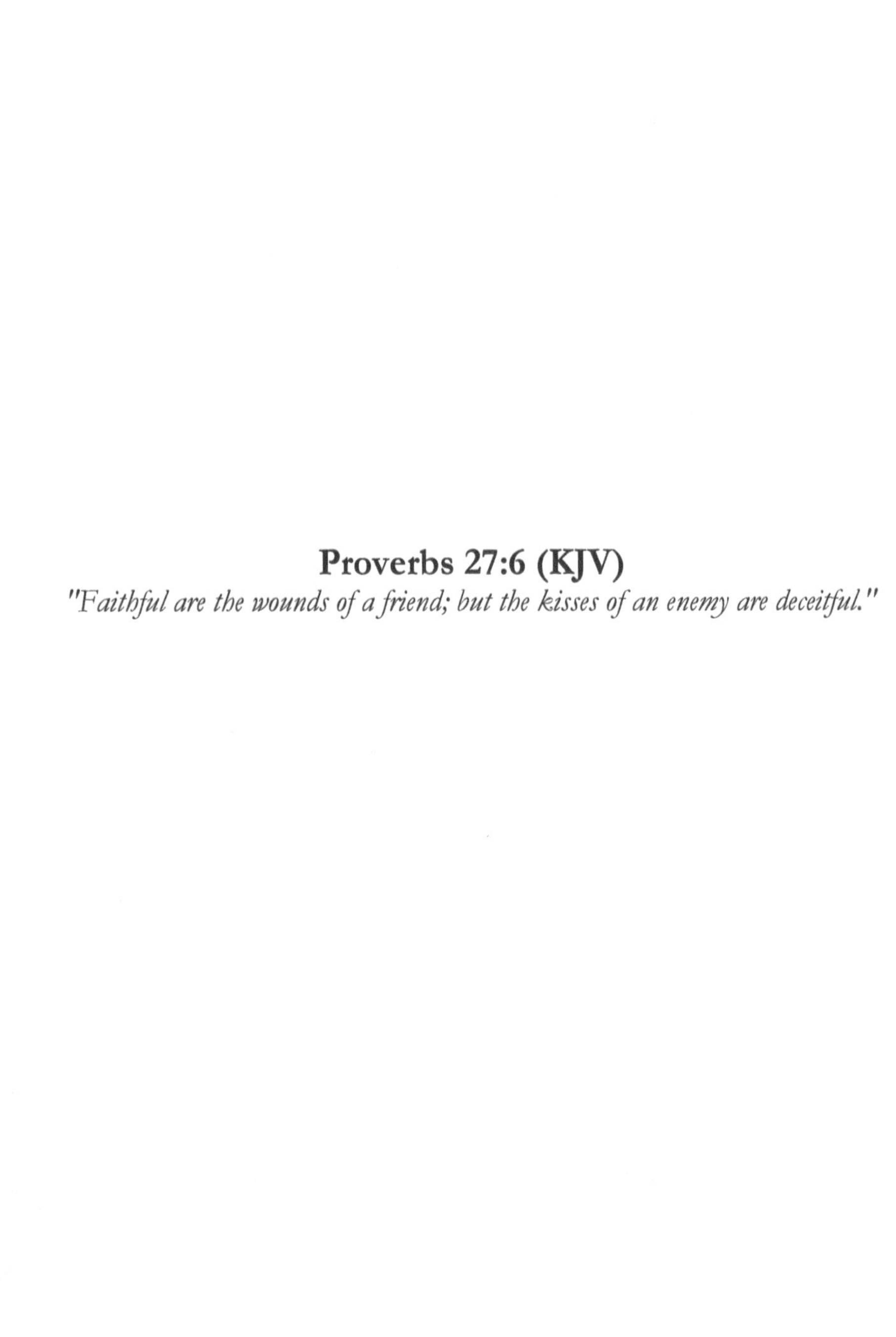

Proverbs 27:6 (KJV)
"Faithful are the wounds of a friend; but the kisses of an enemy are deceitful."

"You Are Not Small"

They say they love, then tear apart,
A smile that hides a sharpened heart.
Their words are like knives, they twist and turn,
You stand in flames, and still they burn.

They mock your tears, they dim your light,
They make the day feel like night.
Control the steps your feet may take,
And paint you wrong for your own sake.

They speak in thunder, rage, and blame,
Then swear that you're the one insane.
They shift the truth, deny the sting,
Gaslight your soul, break everything.

But hear this truth, let silence fall:
You are not weak. You are not small.
Their power lies in smoke and fear,
But every lie will soon grow clear.

A person's love should lift you high,
Not cage your wings, or watch you cry.
Respect is not a game or guise
It meets you whole, it does not lie.

You didn't make them twist the truth,
Or crush the joy you had in youth.
Their hurt began before they met
Your kindness, but you don't owe debt.

You're not the cure for what they hide,
Not made to weather every tide.
It's not your job to break or bend,
To bleed yourself just to defend.

So, hold your ground, reclaim your name,
This isn't love its power and shame.
Step through the smoke, don't close your eyes,
Your truth is strong, and love won't lie.

And if you doubt, or feel alone,
Let these words echo through your bones:
You're not imagining the fall
You're not too much. You are not small.

Isaiah 54:17 (KJV)

"No weapon that is formed against thee shall prosper; and every tongue that shall rise against thee in judgment thou shalt condemn. This is the heritage of the servants of the Lord, and their righteousness is of me, saith the Lord."

"The Cart Game"

I walked through aisles, the grocery store,
Pushing the cart, the routine's a bore,
But then you paused, and with a sigh,
Said, "This cart's broken, I'll have to try."

You went for another, I stood and waited,
Your strange behavior, I truly hated.
You stood at the entrance, like I'd been wrong,
As if the clock ticked on too long.

I walked away, no need to stay,
But then you called me, "We've been waiting all day!"
Your voice, it was sharp, your tone so tight,
Like I was the cause of this petty fight.

You said I'd left, like I had strayed,
Yet I was the one who'd been delayed.
Your words, they twisted, pulled me around,
Making me question what I had found.

An excuse for the cart? A story to tell,
Distracting me from the truth so well.
I questioned myself, felt guilt and shame,
Forgetting your tricks, your twisted game.

"You've kept us waiting," you said with ease,
Making me feel like I was the tease.
But it was your actions, the stand at the door,
That held me back, kept me from the floor.

You shifted the blame, turned it around,
Trying to make me feel like I'd let you down.
But the truth's clear now, I see through the play,
It's all about control, your twisted way.

So, here's the truth, the rhyme, the call,
It's not about me; it's not my fall.
Your game is old, your moves are worn,

But I'll rise above, no longer torn.

In this grocery store, you won't control,
My actions, my heart, my very soul.
Your tricks are weak, they're just a show,
But I'll walk away and let it go.

Proverbs 26:28 (KJV)
"A lying tongue hateth those that are afflicted by it; and a flattering mouth worketh ruin."

The Weight of Trust (and Other Unusual Things)

In midnight's grip, beneath a starless dome,
A call rang out, far from hearth and home.
Not mother's voice, nor father's calm appeal,
But to your partner came the spinning wheel.

A worker, caught in chaos, stress, and strife,
Tangled deep in the thorns of private life.
Why not call kin, whose love should always stay?
Why reach for bosses when the hearts astray?

Perhaps he saw a steadiness so rare,
A lighthouse through a storm he couldn't bear.
A work-bound bond, a trust he couldn't name,
That flickered like a candle in shame.

He spoke of fights and flashing lights,
Of shelters cold and long forgotten rights.
He spoke of jobs as though they were shore,
A place to stand when he could take no more.

But here's the twist that makes the gut go cold
The story's cracked, not all of it feels told.
When truths are stitched with chaos and regret,
We start to wonder what we should forget.

Did panic choose your partner for the plea?
Or was it planned a quiet strategy?
When drama grows and logic takes a dive,
We sense the spin and start to feel alive
To danger, guilt, or manipulation's thread,
Things are not spoken, but so loudly said.

And now you sit with questions in your hand,
Unsure if trust was built on shifting sand.
But doubts don't bloom from nowhere in the air
They root where instincts whisper, "This feels rare."

So, ask yourself Is this a onetime call?
Or has the weight been shifting all along the wall?
A shelter not just built of stone or wood

It's made of who we trust and what we should.

42

Proverbs 3:5-6 (KJV)

"Trust in the Lord with all thine heart; and lean not unto thine own understanding. In all thy ways acknowledge him, and he shall direct thy paths."

Low Self-Esteem
(A Poem on the Hidden Storms of Insecurity)

Walks through life with shoulders low,
Afraid to let the true self show.
Questions about every move that's made,
And fears that each step brings a blade.

The mirror speaks in cruel disguise,
Distorting truth before the eyes.
Worth and value feel so small,
A quiet fight to stand at all.

Seeks a nod, a word, a smile
Validation for a while.
Without it, storms of doubt begin,
And silence howls beneath the skin.

When love is near, becomes unsure,
Afraid such warmth will not endure.
Clings too tight, or pulls away,
In fear that hearts will never stay.

A word, a glance, a passing jest
Can turn to fire in the chest.
Braces hard for any blow,
Though hurt runs deeper than it shows.

Won't take the leap, avoid the fall,
Too scared to risk, too weak to call.
Dreams collected in dusty drawers,
Behind regret and bolted doors.

To mask the cracks, put on a show,
Boasts and brags with practiced glow.
Yet underneath that loud display,
Lies fear just waiting to decay.

When love knocks gently at the gate,
Withdraws in silence, fears too late.

To bare the soul feels far too raw
So, walls go up and love grows small.
Moods may swing from bright to bleak,
A steady voice feels hard to seek.
Confusion grows among the crowd,
Who wondered why it was loud, then bowed.

Please all to earn a place,
Neglects own needs to save some face.
Twists and bends to fit the mold,
As self-respect gets undersold.

A voice inside repeats the lie:
"Not enough, don't even try."
Questions bloom like choking vines,
Each thought a trap, each doubt aligns.

Thoughts replay like worn-out tracks,
Future fears and haunted cracks.
The present fades in anxious blur,
While "what if's" constantly recur.

Brushes off a kind remark,
As if such praise must miss the mark.
Shrinks beneath a compliment,
Though truth in it was clearly meant.

Grasps at titles, roles, and looks,
Identity built out of hooks.
Yet even wealth or beauty's gleam
Can't satisfy the buried scream.

Psalm 139:14 (KJV)

"I will praise thee; for I am fearfully and wonderfully made: marvellous are thy works; and that my soul knoweth right well."

"While I Was Sleeping"

While I was sleeping, you came to life,
No weight of worry, no hint of strife.
Eyes wide open, a secret flame,
Yet when I rise, you're not the same.

You lie so still when I'm awake,
As if my presence makes you break.
Pretending to slumber to build a wall,
But I've heard the silence call.

You bloom in hours I do not see,
A different man when free from me.
Your comfort hides in veils of night,
As if I dim your inner light.

I reach for closeness, soft and true,
But shadows stretch between us two.
And though our bodies share a bed,
There're oceans swirling in your head

A whisper caught in lips you seal,
A love you're scared to touch or feel.
What are you hiding deep inside
A fear of loss, a wound, a pride?

The truth lies quiet in your breath,
More haunting than the ghost of death.
I see peace when I'm not near,
And feel replaced by quiet fear.

Is this escape or just your way
To feel the sun when skies are gray?
Do I demand too much, too loud
Or do I simply break your cloud?

Yet still I stay and softly speak,
Though answers drift and questions leak.
I long to meet the man you are
When I'm asleep beneath the stars.
So, tell me, love, if you can see

A life where you wake up with me
No walls, no masks, no dream to feign,
Just open eyes through joy and pain.
For love is not a game of hide,
It's meeting hearts where truths abide.
And if you're there behind the veil
Come speak to me, and not the pale.

1 John 4:18 (KJV)

*"There is no fear in love; but perfect love casteth out fear: because fear hath torment.
He that feareth is not made perfect in love."*

"We Signed in Silent Ink"

We built a dream on paper ground,
But now your silence is the loudest sound.
Three days you held what I did not,
A paper unsigned, a tangled plot.

I told you quickly, no pause, no game,
But you just stared and passed the blame.
You said, "Why not include me too?"
But you had days before I knew.

You gaslit soft with shifting tone,
Denied your words I heard alone.
You swore you never said that thing
The class reunion, sans my ring.

Confusion brewed behind your eyes,
And every truth wore thin disguise.
I wondered Did you tell a friend,
Or plot a story with an end?

A paper, a lie, a strange delay,
A plan you kept tucked far away.
And yet you spin it back on me
"Why didn't we look jointly?"

Control in quiet hands you keep,
While I lose trust and lose my sleep.
I second guess what once felt clear,
Now clouded thick with doubt and fear.

You shift the weight you will not bear,
I lift your guilt from vacant air.
You disengage, retract your touch,
And act as if I asked too much.

But love should be a space to grow,
Not one where secrets softly flow.
A lease means more than time or place

It speaks of trust, of shared embrace.

Yet here we are two silent pens,
One writes the truth, one just pretends.
And if you plan to walk alone,
Why build this house, not just a home?

I'm not the fool, I'm not the flaw
I gave you truth, I gave you law.
But now I see what's real.
You fear the bond that you might feel.

So, here's your key, and here's the light,
I won't stay lost inside this tonight.
I'll sign my name with heart and grace,
And find a life in a safer place.

Amos 3:3 (KJV)
"Can two walk together, except they be agreed?"

"The Blame Game"

In the stillness of the room, a cloud begins to grow,
A whisper of dissatisfaction that no one seems to know.
He says, "I'm kind of sad," a comment that feels tight,
But deeper lies a story, concealed from the light.

He chose not to do, yet his sadness lays at your door,
As if his decision to step back wasn't something he swore.
The blame comes softly, wrapped in passive aggression's tone,
A hidden message behind words, though the truth's overthrown.

He projects his guilt, like shadows cast on the wall,
As if his actions weren't his, but he alone can't recall.
Shifting blame and turning tears into a tale untold,
The victim's mask he wears, in the silence growing cold.

A dance of guilt, a rhythm of blame that doesn't end,
Where words don't heal but push the heart to bend.
What's lost in the air, the communication so skewed,
Is a need for truth, and honesty pursued.

But here's the key, for both hearts to break free,
A conversation, real and raw, is the key to clarity.
Instead of twisting tales in the darkened night,
Speak out the truth, embrace what's right.

Let go of the blame, the guilt that weighs so deep,
Acknowledge choices, and no more secrets to keep.
For in the light of honesty, the blame can fade,
And love, once clouded, can finally be made.

Galatians 6:5 (KJV)
"For every man shall bear his own burden."

"Echoes of Manipulation"

When your voice rises high, and they hum it away,
It's a signal that your feelings may not hold sway.
They drown out your words with that soft, airy tune,
Trying to downplay your emotions, like a dark afternoon.

A picture from years past, a moment in time,
To trigger nostalgia, and make you rewind.
They whisper, "Remember when we used to be close?"
But it's not love they're after it's control they boast.

"Remember, I've always wanted you," they say,
A plea to make you forget how they push you away.
With a flick of the wrist, they shift the past's light,
But their present behavior just doesn't feel right.

Insecurity's grip, so fragile and near,
They deflect with a smile, while hiding fear.
Narcissism's dance, on a thin thread of pride,
Afraid of your leaving, they want you beside.

Emotional immaturity, they choose to avoid,
Facing the conflict, they're too paranoid.
With nostalgia and guilt, they try to entrap,
Turning your feelings into an emotional trap.

But you stand tall, don't let them stray,
Your boundaries are firm; you won't be led astray.
Manipulation's trick you've learned to see,
Their echoes of silence won't control you, or me.

Remember the pattern, the past's warm embrace,
Can't erase the truth with their clever grace.
Evaluate what's real, not just what's been sold,
For love should be gentle, not ice cold and bold.

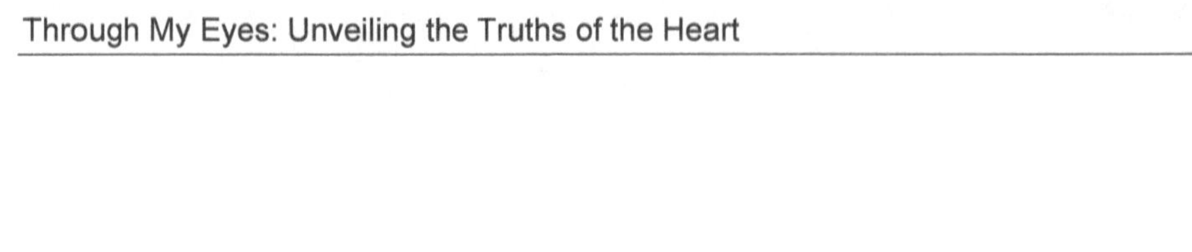

Proverbs 26:24-25 (KJV)

"He that hateth dissembleth with his lips, and layeth up deceit within him; When he speaketh fair, believe him not: for there are seven abominations in his heart."

"The Recipe of Blame"

He sighs and says with downcast tone,
"I'm kind of sad I didn't do that."
But wait, didn't he choose that path?
Now I'm the one who feels his wrath.

He speaks in riddles, hints, and sighs,
Hiding truth behind tired eyes.
It wasn't me who let that slip,
Yet I'm caught in the blame filled grip.

I never do that anymore. Is what he says
You chose not to, is what I said
Yet somehow now it's all on me.
A dance of guilt, a silent plea,
But the choice was his, can't you see?

It's projection, a twisted game,
He hides behind his own self-blame.
A passive-aggressive, subtle strike,
That paints me wrong though I'm not alike.

"Why don't you do that?" the words are near,
But never quite crystal clear.
The truth is buried, veiled in doubt,
As if his choices don't count.

He's the victim, or so he seems,
Drowning in his own lost dreams.
I'm caught between the lines of care,
But where's the truth in what we share?

Each sighs a mask, each word a trap,
I'm caught in webs of his misstep.
His sadness, though real, is not mine,
But still he's spinning it all on time.

Oh, if he'd speak the honest plea,
"I haven't done that; it's up to me."
Then we'd both breathe, a common space,
Without guilt he tries to place.

For in this dance, this twisted rhyme,
He hides behind his own lost time.
But I can't fix what's not my fault,
He's the one who holds the halt.

So let him own his choices, true,
And I'll own mine, what's there to do?
For in this game of guilt and blame,
The truth remains, untouched by shame.

Ezekiel 18:20 (KJV)

"The soul that sinneth, it shall die. The son shall not bear the iniquity of the father, neither shall the father bear the iniquity of the son: the righteousness of the righteous shall be upon him, and the wickedness of the wicked shall be upon him."

"The Stranger in My Celebration"

On the night that bore my name in light,
I hoped for joy, warm hugs, delights
But something in the air turned thin,
A shadow crept its way within.

They planned a dinner, sweet and grand,
My man, my friend, a joint command.
Yet where were those I held so near?
The ones who'd cheer me year after year?

"My sister couldn't come," they said,
"My cousin, too" the line felt dead.
Excuses whispered, soft and sly,
But silence doesn't always lie.

She leaned in close, too close to him,
A look, a touch, a secret hymn.
Her children there, unasked, in tow
A birthday turned into a private show.

She smiled and asked for him alone,
To fetch her wine in undertone.
And though my name was on the night,
It felt like she had claimed the light.

I wandered off to hide my tears,
The weight of silence in my ears.
The restaurant bathroom caught my pain,
Where joy should dance, now grief remains.

A moment lost, a wound too deep,
That night still lingers in my sleep.
For what is love, when lines are blurred,
And friends speak soft but act absurdly?

A partner should shield, not share your throne.
Respect in private must be shown.
When someone leans too far, too fast,

It's not just past it may not pass.

Boundaries shattered don't heal clean,
Your soul sensed what was in between.
Your tears were not from petty pride,
But from being pushed to the side

A friend who isolates your cheer
May crave control or play on fear.
Projection, envy, subtle war
Unhealed hearts can still want more.

You saw the cracks; you took a stand.
Your feelings? Valid. Deep. Alive.
Your pain tells stories you'll survive.

So, stand up tall, reclaim your throne
Let no one steal your joy for long
For love is yours, both bright and true
And real friends never outshine you.

Proverbs 27:6 (KJV)

"Faithful are the wounds of a friend; but the kisses of an enemy are deceitful."

"Whispers in the Inbox"

We welcomed our child, a moment so grand,
A new little heartbeat held soft in our hand.
But shadows creep where the sunlight should stay,
A whisper arrived in a curious way.

A friend of mine or so I had thought
Reached out to him with the message she brought.
No text to me, no joyous call,
Just slid in his inbox, not mine at all.

"Congratulations," her message read,
He showed me the words that her fingers had said.
Phone in his palm, no secrets to keep,
But my stomach sank and my peace lost sleep.

Why not to both of us why just to him?
This moment of joy now clouded and dim.
Not a post, not a call, not even a text,
Just a private salute that left me perplexed.

We've been through decades, twenty-five years,
Through laughter and heartache, and buckets of tears.
Yet now in the glow of this newborn light,
She chose a path that just didn't sit right.

What was her motive? What was her goal?
Why bypass the mother, the heart and the soul?
A woman, postpartum, raw to the core,
And a friend that I trusted I trusted no more.

A coach might say Define your lines,
Where loyalty ends and where respect shines.
Were your expectations ever made clear?
Or did silent assumptions live year after year?"

A therapist might gently pull at the thread,
"Is this one cut, or old wounds that bled?
What hurt has she triggered, what grief sits beneath?
And what's wrapped in silence, behind your teeth?"

A psychologist might map out your brain,
And trace this confusion to lingering pain.
Could hormones be swirling? Could history repeat?
Does this boundary breach a past incomplete?

But none of their titles, their letters or frames,
Can soften the echo that quietly blames.
You should feel seen. You should feel heard.
And this felt like poison disguised as a word.

Perhaps it was clumsy, or maybe unkind,
But her choice cut deep through the roots of your mind.
This wasn't just a misplaced hello
It was the absence of you in the place where it should go.

Now trust feels broken, shattered in two,
And grieving a friendship is heavy but true.
Not every goodbye comes with a sound,
Sometimes it's silence that lays you down.

So, guard your heart, new mother so brave,
You've life to nourish and joy to save.
Let her explain, or let her fade,
But you choose how your peace is made.

For friends should lift and never confuse
And if they make you question, it's your right to choose.
Because love should include you, not hide you away.
Not whisper to him what they should freely say.

Proverbs 4:23 (KJV)
"Keep thy heart with all diligence; for out of it are the issues of life."

"The Cap and the Question"

Twenty-five years, a long friendship,
Through highs and lows, we both stayed strong.
She called me close on her big day,
"I've got a favor, if I may."

She said, "I didn't tell you school was the plan,
I had to be sure I knew I can."
I smiled so wide, my heart was full,
Proud of her rise, her quiet pull.

"I'll do your cap," I said with pride,
With colors bold and stars that glide.
A canvas crowned in joy and grace,
A milestone marked with love in place.

But then she asked odd questions,
One that left me feeling flawed
"Did your partner see what you designed?
Tell him I'm getting my life aligned."

It caught me off a gentle sting,
Why was he the one this spring?
This day was hers, and I stood near,
A friend who held her dreams so dear.

Why seek his eyes on such a feat?
Why not just dance in your own beat?
Was this a need to be admired,
By someone else I hadn't hired.

She speaks of him too much, too free,
As if he sits between her and me.
Approval sought where none was due,
In shadows cast where light once grew.

Someone might say, "She seeks a place,
In hierarchies she can't erase."
A wise man could find the thread

Old wounds or words left long unsaid.

A wise woman might call it need for more,
Validation knocking at the door.
Not from my loyal friend
But from the man I did not lend.

Was this a game, a test, a cry?
To measure worth through someone's eye?
And in that moment, all felt skewed,
The joy, the bond, the gratitude.

Still, I was there through all the years,
Through growth and dreams and quiet tears.
But now I see with clearer view,
The layers friendship sometimes grew.

The cap I made still caught the light,
But shadows flickered in my sight.
Not every question is what it seems
Some stem from cracks behind the dreams.

So, here's to love, to truth, to grace,
To know every friendship's place.
Some things we give without regret
But some small questions we don't forget.

"Lines Drawn in Silence"

In circles once golden, now tarnished and thin,
Where laughter once echoed, the cracks now begin.
A friend crossed a line, and the rest simply watched,
Their silence, a dagger so quiet, so botched.

The years we invested, the memories we built,
Now hang in the balance of silence and guilt.
No voices defended, no justice was heard,
Just eyes that looked down and lips that deterred.

You stood by and wavered while wrong took the floor,
Afraid of the ripple, you opened no door.
But peace without truth is a war in disguise,
And silence, my friends, can be treason in ties.

He joked, he encroached, and you chose to pretend
But harm wears a grin when it's cloaked as a friend.
I watched you do nothing and felt the divide,
A storm in my chest that I no longer hide.

I grieve what I thought, what we once used to be,
A compass of loyalty shattered, I see.
But pain is a teacher, and now I am clear,
The ones who stay quiet are loud in my ear.

So here are my lines, both gentle and bold,
My love may be warm, but my spine will hold.
I won't play a game where respect is denied,
Where wrongs are just shadows that no one will chide.

To the friend who betrayed, and the ones who stood by,
I see with new eyes, and I won't justify.
I'll speak, I'll protect, and I'll rise from this pain,
With values intact in the sun or the rain.

For love without courage is fragile at best,
And friendship without truth will fail every test.
So, here's my goodbye to illusions once dear,

I'm choosing my peace, and I'm drawing it clear.

Proverbs 31:8 (KJV)
"Open thy mouth for the dumb in the cause of all such as are appointed to destruction."

"The Mirror Cracked"

It all began with shattered glass,
A reckless move, then came the sass
"I wish my cost weren't quite so steep,"
Yet deeper truths began to creep.

A sigh, a shrug, a fleeting frown
But something darker held its ground.
Not just mistake, but veiled regret,
A weight of envy quietly set.

You rose from wreckage, calm and still,
While silence echoed power and will.
And yet, a jab, a subtle cue
A need to prove more strength than you.

The blame was shifted, words were spun,
Avoiding truths that can't outrun.
No nod to what you had endured,
Just burdens claimed and self-assured.

Your pain dismissed, the air grew thick,
While ego played its oldest trick.
No empathy, no open gaze
Just self-concern in tangled praise.

Still, you stand, though spirit worn,
By love that leaves the heart forlorn.
A bond that muffles what you feel,
Where "care" no longer seems quite real.

So, ask yourself in quiet light:
What do you crave in love at night?
To feel at home, to breathe with ease,
To trust, to heal, to find release.

What signs would show you're truly seen
Not masked in charm, but clear, serene?
What truths must hold, what must not bend,

When breaking feels like it won't end?

Imagine joy that isn't guessed,
A steady peace, a soul at rest.
Where every need met with respect,
And love is more than just a check.

Now look once more, and ask what's true:
Is hope what keeps this tied to you?
Or is it fear that grips so tight,
While dreams of "more" still stir at night?

A love that drains and leaves you bare
Is not a cross you're meant to wear.
You're meant for more than just to cope
You're meant for love that stokes your hope.

So, ask again, and let truth say
Does this love build you day by day?
Or is it time to walk alone
Toward light, toward peace, toward your own home?

John 8:32 (KJV)
"And ye shall know the truth, and the truth shall make you free."

"The Last Night"

I showed up late, heart full of dread,
Already knowing where this night had led.
My game night, yes but not for me,
They played their part so openly.

She left the room just her and him,
No shame, no pause, no sense of sin.
I'd said before, "This crosses lines,"
But still they laughed, their hearts aligned.

They moved in sync, a silent code,
A private path, a secret road.
He didn't look at me that night,
His gaze at her and his grip held tight.

No call, no text while I was out,
Just silence, thick with rising doubt.
But in that store, I found strange peace,
A breath, a pause, a brief release.

Then home I came, the vibe was wrong,
A place I built, but don't belong.
My 20-year friend, too drunk to walk,
And suddenly, it's late-night talk.

"Take care of her," my friend had said
But what about me? The tears I bled.
Why was she not up with me?
Why was he there, where would she be?

She slept downstairs, he stayed down too,
Like I was ghost, not flesh and true.
My voice was lost, my soul dismissed,
A partner's touch I hadn't kissed.

I watched them with a wounded eye,
And wondered why I even tried.
Is this love, or some cruel joke,
Where is trust burned and never spoke?

I gave my heart, I gave my time,
But now I taste betrayal crime.
You held her more than you held me
You made her feel what I should be.

So here I stand, and here I break,
A woman scorned, wide eyed awake.
No more games, no silent screams,
I'm walking out, reclaiming dreams.

For love is truth, not silent theft
And this was the last game night left.

Psalm 55:12-14, 22 (KJV)

"For it was not an enemy that reproached me; then I could have borne it: neither was it he that hated me that did magnify himself against me; then I would have hid myself from him:
But it was thou, a man mine equal, my guide, and mine acquaintance.
We took sweet counsel together, and walked unto the house of God in company."

"Sacred Space"

Thank you for bearing the truth of your soul,
When pain tells a tale, it must be told whole.
It's deeper than anger, it's sharper than fear
When someone you love is the one who won't hear.

In moments so fragile, postpartum and bare,
You needed soft hands and someone to care for.
But instead came betrayal, a snapshot, a theft
Of stillness and laughter, and all that was left.

When someone keeps stepping where they don't belong,
It's not just a mistake it's a pattern gone wrong.
Is it about power? Is it control?
Or simply a man who's lost in his role?

Does he stand by you, or twist every thread?
Do you feel safe when you climb into bed?
Has he learned consent, or just walked away
When you asked him to see you, did he choose to stay?

Did he treat your truths with the care they were due,
Or scatter them wide with no thought about you?
That's not just a moment that's ripping a seam,
That's crushing the quiet inside of a dream.

So, name what you know. Don't soften the blow.
Are your needs respected? Just tell him "No."
Does he grow with your growth, or stand in your way?
You deserve more than surviving the day.

You are divine crafted deep from the stars,
Wounded, yet radiant, bearing your scars.
If his very presence dims your own light,
Then rise from the shadows and step into right.

This is your temple, your body, your breath,
Not a space for neglect, not a stage for regret.
Guard it with fire, with mercy, with might

Let no one profane what is sacred and bright.
You've spent too long unseen and unheard,
But you hold the ending, the start, every word.
The power is yours it always has been
To close every door, he broke open within.

For love is not silence, or guilt laced delay
It's choosing each other, in truth, every day.
And if he won't shield your most tender part,
Then let you be the one who honors your heart.

1 Corinthians 6:19-20 (KJV)

"What? know ye not that your body is the temple of the Holy Ghost which is in you, which ye have of God, and ye are not your own?
For ye are bought with a price: therefore glorify God in your body, and in your spirit, which are God's."

"The Mirror You Tried to Break"

You told me I was all your skies,
But love is proven not in lies.
You held me close, then walked away,
Said all was fine, then made me pay.

You whispered truths you later bent,
Gaslighted every moment spent.
The past was twisted, torn apart
You blurred my mind to break my heart.

You'd shout, then say it's just a joke,
Leave love behind in ash and smoke.
The ring you claimed was mine to keep
A threat now dangled when I weep.

You watched her walk, you met her gaze,
Then blamed me for my doubtful phase.
Your praise was loud, your silence deep
Your loyalty was yours to cheat.

You'd cage me close, then lock the door,
Demanding more while giving poor.
You'd starve me for your truth, your time
Then paint my questions as a crime.

Control disguised as deep concern,
Affection is used as twist and turn.
I shrunk myself to fit your mold,
Yet still, your heart remains ice cold.

But I see through the smoke and spin
This war was never mine to win.
You fought to feel like you were whole
By stealing pieces of my soul.

And now I rise, no longer blind,
Your power lies in what I find:
That truth is quiet, clear, and bright
And I am walking toward the light.

Isaiah 54:17 (KJV)

"No weapon that is formed against thee shall prosper; and every tongue that shall rise against thee in judgment thou shalt condemn. This is the heritage of the servants of the Lord, and their righteousness is of me, saith the Lord

"Lurching or Tugging at the Ear"

Lurching or tugging at the ear,
A silent sign when truth's not nearby,
Not proof of lies, but something stirred,
A feeling felt, though never heard.

A glance away, a shifting stance,
A hurried word, a fleeting glance.
They raise their voice, then throw their hands
But drama's not where truth often stands.

For lies don't always wear a mask,
Nor shout aloud the guilty task.
They dance in gaps, in tales too neat,
In what's avoided, in retreat.

He says he's done no whispering deed,
Yet somehow plants a mother's seed
Her words cut sharp, her gaze is cold,
A judgment cast, both young and old.

You speak your hurt, he dodges blame,
A pattern drawn from shame to shame.
The promises, once warm, now chill,
You climb a slope; he stands there still.

And every tear, and every fight,
Is shadowed by what isn't right
Not just the facts, but what they lack
A heart that stands and has your back.

Is it defense, or some deceit?
A tangled web, too worn, repeat.
You beg for truth, not grand display,
Just calm, clear words that choose to stay.

But still he flares, then folds in tears,
Each storm confirms all your fears.
Not always lies but something breaks

When love just gives but never takes.

So, if he flinches when you cry,
Or shouts so he won't have to try
Know this: the truth is soft, not loud,
It doesn't hide behind a crowd.

Your child sees more than either say,
In silence shaped by each new day.
She needs a world where love is clear
Not one that tugs upon the ear.

Ecclesiastes 5:2 (KJV)

"Be not rash with thy mouth, and let not thine heart be hasty to utter any thing before God: for God is in heaven, and thou upon earth: therefore let thy words be few."

"Why Have All Our Moments Stopped?"

Why have all our moments stopped?
Who did you give them up for?
On sunny days we stay indoors,
And rainy days just weigh us more.

Our children laugh in borrowed light,
Afraid to shine, to play, to be
Because you fear the world might see
The life you live with them and me.

No museums, no parks, no shows,
No nighttime walks where true love grows.
No dinner dates, no weekend plans,
Just hiding hearts and folded hands.

Why am I your shadow's ghost?
A secret tucked away the most.
Only at night, in dim lit screens,
Am I allowed to share your dreams.

But love is light. It needs to shine.
Not only yours it must be mine.
I will not stay locked in the door,
My children will not suffer more.

I'll strap my shoes, I'll lift my face,
I'll fill my world with joy and grace.
We'll find the sunlight we've been owed,
No longer walking this hidden road.

So, take your secrets, your delay,
Your restaurant towns so far away.
I want the now, not some excuse,
Not love that hides or feels like truce.

We got together and I was proud.
But you still whisper, never loud.
While I've been screaming in my soul,
Deserving more than half, not whole.

I choose the better, loud and clear.
Our joy will bloom, not disappear.
I rise for love that's real and wide
Not just what's tucked away to hide.

Luke 8:16 (KJV)

"No man, when he hath lighted a candle, covereth it with a vessel, or putteth it under a bed; but setteth it on a candlestick, that they which enter in may see the light."

"Lines Drawn in Silence"

In circles once golden, now tarnished and thin,
Where laughter once echoed, the cracks now begin.
A friend crossed a line, and the rest simply watched,
Their silence, a dagger so quiet, so botched.

The years we invested, the memories we built,
Now hang in the balance of silence and guilt.
No voices defended, no justice was heard,
Just eyes that looked down and lips that deterred.

You stood by and wavered while wrong took the floor,
Afraid of the ripple, you opened no door.
But peace without truth is a war in disguise,
And silence, my friends, can be treason in ties.

He joked, he encroached, and you chose to pretend
But harm wears a grin when it's cloaked as a friend.
I watched you do nothing and felt the divide,
A storm in my chest that I no longer hide.

I grieve what I thought, what we once used to be,
A compass of loyalty shattered, I see.
But pain is a teacher, and now I am clear,
The ones who stay quiet are loud in my ear.

So here are my lines, both gentle and bold,
My love may be warm, but my spine will hold.
I won't play a game where respect is denied,
Where wrongs are just shadows that no one will chide.

To the friend who betrayed, and the ones who stood by,
I see with new eyes, and I won't justify.
I'll speak, I'll protect, and I'll rise from this pain,
With values intact in the sun or the rain.

For love without courage is fragile at best,
And friendship without truth will fail every test.
So, here's my goodbye to illusions once dear,

I'm choosing my peace, and I'm drawing it clear.

Psalm 41:9 (KJV)

"Yea, mine own familiar friend, in whom I trusted, which did eat of my bread, hath lifted up his heel against me."

"Rebirth"

It began with a gaze, not a kiss, but a clue,
A lesson in shadows I once called true.
But storms birth stars, and now I view
The path I walked as wisdom's due.

You came like fire, dressed as fate,
But I've learned to love what trials create.
You shaped a space I now translate
Into strength no wound can be replicated.

I bled, yes but bleeding made me bloom,
I found my light inside the gloom.
I dusted joy from sorrow's room,
And painted peace where pain once loomed.

Not all who touch are meant to stay,
Some teach by tearing dreams away.
But every loss has cleared the way
For brighter dawns and kinder days.

I let you in, but I let me go
Now I reclaim the soul I know.
I've shed the weight, unlearned the show,
And planted seeds from scars that grow.

You were the lesson, not the doom,
A wilted rose that made more room.
I built new roots from your perfume,
Now life is in full bloom.

You weren't my fate you were my fire,
That burned the cage, then climbed it higher.
But smoke can't smother pure desire
It only proves the soul's entirety.

So, thank you, love, for what you cost,
For every piece I thought was lost.
You broke me just to melt the frost

And showed me I was never tossed.

I rise with grace, no need for war,
My silence speaks what screams before.
You were a chapter, nothing more
I've closed that book and found my core.

Now I dance, not for your view,
But for the dawn and skies more true.
This isn't hate its life anew.
I found myself when I lost you.

Romans 8:28 (KJV)

"And we know that all things work together for good to them that love God, to them who are the called according to his purpose."

"The Seat They Left Empty"

I waited with hope, heart open and wide,
But they never came, though I stood outside.
Three friends I had trusted for many a year,
Vanished like ghosts, leaving silence and fear.

The show had begun, so I bought my own place,
Hoping to glimpse a familiar face.
But they sat together, laughing in line,
While I sat alone, pretending I'm fine.

The curtain had dropped, and the night was still young,
They mentioned a meal; their hunger had sprung.
So, I drove through the dark with a flutter of cheer,
To a place where I thought they'd soon appear.

But minutes turned hours, and no one came,
Just messages saying they'd chosen a name
A different spot, no mention to me,
Left in the shadows, abandoned to be.

Alone at a table in cold city light,
Scared of the darkness that haunted the night.
Not just the streets that were empty and bare,
But the hearts of the friends who once used to care.

It cut like a blade, not just skin but soul,
A wound unseen yet taking its toll.
My mind played the questions on repeat inside
Why did they leave me? Why had they lied?

Did they not value the bond we had made?
Or was my worth something easy to trade?
This wasn't the first time they'd left me behind,
A pattern of silence, cold and unkind.

My needs weren't met, my heart wasn't heard,
Their actions spoke louder than any word.
Support turned to weight the day I got rings,
Since then, friendship has fractured in things.

But out of this aching, I started to see,
There's strength in the stillness that blossomed in me.
For Jesus, my Friend, stood steady and true,
In places where people just wouldn't come through.

My soul now seeks more than their fleeting praise,
It longs for a path with purpose and grace.
To be seen, to be safe, to be deeply known
By friends who don't leave me out there alone.

So, I honor the tears and the stories they tell,
They speak of a hurt I remember too well.
But also of healing, of rising anew,
Of cutting old ties so that love can break through.

To those who once mattered, I bid you goodbye,
No anger, just truth and a well learned sigh.
This seat you left empty now holds my own light
And I won't dim again just to make others right.

Deuteronomy 31:6 (KJV)

"Be strong and of a good courage, fear not, nor be afraid of them: for the Lord thy God, he it is that doth go with thee; he will not fail thee, nor forsake thee."

"A Mirror, not a Map"

Why do you chase what they create,
As if their steps define our fate.
A garden grows, you want one too,
But is it ours or just their view?

You watch their world through filtered glass,
Then plant their past within our grass.
You mirror moves they choose to make,
But is it real, or just opaque?

Do you still see her in your mind,
A chapter lost you seek to find.
Or is it him the life he shows
That stirs the ache you never chose.

Is this a race you're running still,
To prove you've climbed your own new hill.
Or just a need to feel secure,
By copying what seems so sure?

But love, our life is not a show,
No need to echo where they go.
Let's build from dreams that we define,
Not borrowed shapes or past design.

Let's ask not what the world would do,
But what feels good and true for you.
And if you're lost, I'll hold your hand,
While side by side, we learn to stand.

A mirror only shows a face
It can't create a brand-new place.
So, let's stop tracing someone's art
And draw the future from our heart.

Romans 12:2 (KJV)

"And be not conformed to this world: but be ye transformed by the renewing of your mind, that ye may prove what is that good, and acceptable, and perfect, will of God."

"The Day I Left the Chat"

I asked a question, calm and clear,
"What day this weekend? Let me hear."
A simple ask, no hidden tone,
Just wanting plans, not left alone.

Then came a jab, so smooth, so sly
"Well duh, the weekend" was the reply.
The laughing followed, sharp and cold,
Like childhood echoes, growing old.

A person laughed, emojis flew,
As if my voice was nothing new.
A room of kin, but none had seen
The hurt tucked softly in between.

So quietly, I hit "Leave Chat,"
No storm, no scream, just done with that.
A thread that snapped, a choice to go,
To dodge the sting, they'd never know.

They chuckle still, I wouldn't doubt,
While I rebuild from inside out.
Cause silence speaks when words won't land,
And walking out can be a stand.

I've learned to guard what they dismiss,
My questions are born from hope, not his.
It's not a sin to seek time,
Nor weakness just to draw a line.

Each time I leave, it marks a scar,
From battles waged where love should spar.
But leaving's not defeat or shame
It's self-respect. It's staking claim.

So, if they ask, "Why gone so fast?"
Say: Loyalty should always last,
But laughter made at someone's pain

Is not a joke it leaves a stain."

I'm still that person, still those kin,
But not the clown they box me in.
And when they meet this weekend's end,
They'll miss the one who called them "friend."

Proverbs 26:4 (KJV)

"Answer not a fool according to his folly, lest thou also be like unto him."

"You Called It Friendship, I Call It Fire"

She smiled like summer, soft and sweet,
But shadows followed her quiet feet.
She laughed at my life, my love, my name,
And whispered my worth like it was a shame.

She said, "Just your man, just your kid, that's all,"
Like I hadn't stood strong or answered the call.
She mocked me in corners, in silence, in code,
While I paved her pain down my heart like a road.

But now I see her game was clear,
She fed on control; she feasted on fear.
She wanted to keep me alone in the end,
To crown herself queen as my only friend.

She sowed small seeds in innocent ears,
And watered them well with gossip and sneers.
A soft little whisper, a sideways glance
All choreographed in a snake like dance.

Why? I don't know. But I do know this
I offered her love, not a wound she could twist.
I prayed for her joy, I showed up through storms,
While she studied my cracks and reshaped her forms.

This wasn't just petty, this cut to the soul,
An attack on my peace, on my heart's control.
Therapists call it betrayal so real
When a "friend" spins your truth like a wheel.

She needed my light to brighten her void,
But tried to destroy what she couldn't avoid.
She saw my success as a threat, not a win,
So, she tore at the doors I had opened within.

But now, I rise. My clarity's deep.
No more giving gold to those who cheap.
I am the mirror she tried to distort,
Reflecting the power she failed to support.

Spiritually speaking? I'm being refined.
I'm called into circles that feed the divine.
This was a lesson not punishment, no
But proof that I'm growing and ready to grow.

So, here's to the fire she lit in my name,
It forged a new voice and burned off the shame.
I grieve, I release, I will not pretend.
This chapter is closed. She's not my end.

Isaiah 54:17 (KJV)

"No weapon that is formed against thee shall prosper; and every tongue that shall rise against thee in judgment thou shalt condemn. This is the heritage of the servants of the Lord, and their righteousness is of me, saith the Lord."

"The Hanger Wasn't Just a Hanger"

My partner laughs with a humor so sick,
A dagger is disguised as a joke or a trick.
My bridesmaids vanished, one by one,
Since shadows formed where light once shone.

One, I suspect, has crossed a line
Their glances, whispers, far from fine.
The others knew, yet played along,
A silent choir in a traitor's song.

He walked in, holding that hanger of pain,
Like it was just some bridal chain.
But the wedding's off, the dream is dead,
So why bring ghosts back to my bed?

A passive jab wrapped in a grin,
A cruel reminder of what could've been.
Not love, not care, not any grace,
Just power plays masked in my space.

It wasn't a gift, it was a game,
To stir confusion, storm the flame.
A punchline crafted from my cries,
A smile that stings, a love that lies.

I told him plain, "You can put it away
I have no friends left for that day."
He knew the truth, he saw my ache,
But needed proof I wouldn't break.

This isn't humor, its control,
A twisted reach into my soul.
Each move he makes, a test, a gauge,
To keep me trapped inside his cage.

His guilt projected, eyes that shift,
A mind that plays and moods that drift.
He won't confront the things he's done,

He'll joke, he'll twist, he'll simply run.

He's not just joking, it's a disguise,
To blur the truth before my eyes.
But my spirit knows, my heart can feel,
That hanger wasn't fake, it's real.

It held no dresses, no delight,
Just fragments of a stolen night.
A relic from a love betrayed,
A shrine to vows that never stayed.

Spirit says: This is my test
To rise, to leave, to seek what's best.
To see through fog, to cut the cord,
To take my pain and wield my sword.

I'm not insane. I'm not unkind.
I'm simply clear in heart and mind.
The truth's not cruel it's just awake,
And breaking free is mine to take.

The hanger came to stir my soul,
But now I take back control.
I've seen the game, I've read the play,
Now what I choose will light my way.

So, I ask myself with steady breath:
Will I choose rebirth, or choose slow death?
For love is sacred, not joy
And I deserve a life of joy.

Proverbs 4:23 (KJV)

"Keep thy heart with all diligence; for out of it are the issues of life."

"Shower Secrets"

He takes his phone into the spray,
Where water runs and doubts replay.
The steam can't mask the silent signs,
Or hide the guilt between the lines.

The glass is fogged, but not my view,
I see the cracks he's slipping through.
A screen that should be left behind,
It is clutched like secrets in his mind.

He says it's tunes, a podcast stream,
But silence hums beneath the dream.
No laughter echoes through the door,
Just quiet plots I can't ignore.

A message blinks, a screen has gone black,
A smile erased, then turned back.
If nothing hides, then why the haste?
Why rinse the lies but not the taste?

The waterfalls, but so does trust,
Each droplet dull, each moment rust.
For love that's pure won't need disguise,
Nor need a phone where silence lies.

I'm not a fool, I feel the shift,
The space between us starts to drift.
A bath of truth would sting and burn,
But cleanse the soul and let love learn.

So let him scroll, and let him hide,
While I rebuild the heart inside.
The strongest love begins with me
Not secrets drowned in secrecy.

Job 34:21–22 (KJV)

"For his eyes are upon the ways of man, and he seeth all his goings. There is no darkness, nor shadow of death, where the workers of iniquity may hide themselves."

"The Heat Knows Truth"

Beneath the blaze of summer's sun,
Where friendships bloom and secrets run,
The air grew thick with tales untold,
In glances warm, yet strangely cold.

A reel was cast, a silent test,
To see which hearts would beat or rest.
No thumbs, no laughs, no signs, no flame
Just quiet guilt without a name.

You showed your love for the reel's sharp thread,
He flinched and asked what none had said.
"Did they reply?" he dared to ask
A subtle crack within his mask.

The waves don't lie, nor do the skies,
When trust is lost behind the eyes.
The summer knows, the stillness speaks,
Of silent rooms and burning cheeks.

Was it her touch, his shift, their tone?
Or just your heart that felt alone?
But truth, like heat, will rise and bare
What hides beneath will lose its air.

So, hold your strength, your voice, your fire,
Don't dim your light for their desire.
The ones who are wrong, the ones who lie,
Can't steal your stars or claim your sky.

And when the sun sets low and red,
You'll rise above what went unsaid.
For those who stray in passion's flame,
Will one day choke upon the shame.

Numbers 32:23 (KJV)

"But if ye will not do so, behold, ye have sinned against the Lord: and be sure your sin will find you out."

"Through the Quiet, I Knew"

They laughed when I walked out of the room,
Too fast, too close like a subtle bloom.
His eyes would twitch, her breath would stall,
Like secrets clinging to a bedroom wall.

I saw it not in what they said,
But in the way they turned their heads.
The silence roared, the echoes grew,
And through the quiet, I just knew.

A reel I dropped a message bare,
No likes, no laughs, just hollow air.
Their hearts skipped beats in digital space,
Guilt wore calm upon their face.

He asked not "why?" but "who replied?"
A guilty mind too scared to hide.
He didn't flinch at what it meant,
Just checked the room where truth was sent.

She vanished when my world was split,
No hand to hold, no care to sit.
But in front row at my daughter's show,
Still playing friend with face aglow.

Was it care, or just a scan?
To watch us both, to track the plan?
To see if masks would start to slip,
If guilt would crack from her tight grip?

A friend in shadow, love in doubt,
While I am piecing inside out.
If silence speaks, hers screamed too loud,
Betrayal wears a subtle shroud.

So, if you ask me what is true,
I trusted hearts and lost a few.
But broken glass reflects the light,
And I still rise, despite the night.

Let them twist in webs they weave,
I won't beg, and I won't grieve.
I've walked through fire, I've seen the cost
I know what's mine, and what I've lost.

Their truth will rot behind their lies,
But I will bloom where silence dies.
The one they thought would break in two,
Is standing tall and seeing through.

Job 19:19 (KJV)

"All my inward friends abhorred me: and they whom I loved are turned against me."

Last night I was cold and I covered myself.
(May 18,2025)
She was barely freezing, but you covered her. (December)
Today I've come to realize that I'm not covered by you.
Today I have come to realize that I'm deserving to be covered.
Today I have come to realization.
I am covered by the blood of Jesus
Bye blanket.

Revelation 7:14 (KJV)

"...and have washed their robes and made them white in the blood of the Lamb."

"Mirror's Echo"

I read your lines they pierced like blades,
Each verse a flame that never fades.
You paint with pain, yet dress it sweet,
A sin in silk, a drug discreet.

I felt that stare, that soul eclipse,
The venom pouring from his lips.
A siren's hymn, a whispered vice,
A taste of death that feels like spice.

That first hit too I've known that spell,
Were heaven flirts with depths of hell.
Where bodies blend and thoughts distort,
And reason's just a last resort.

I've chased him too through dream and sweat,
A craving carved in my regret.
He fed me highs I couldn't own,
Then left me starving, skin and bone.

Your words, they echo to mine exactly,
This lust, this drug, this binding pact.
Not love no, something more deranged,
A heart's delight, but pre-arranged.

Designer lace, the scent, the tease,
She strips your soul with practice ease.
A phantom dressed in sweet,
But every kiss becomes a tomb.

You said it best a soul tie glue,
A shackle dressed in something new.
I nodded with each line you penned,
For I too loved what had no end.

Your chalice burns I've sipped it too,
And watched my sense dissolve in dew.
Each thrust a debt I still repay,

Each climax is just a price to stay.

He doesn't love he's just a mask,
A pleasure wrapped in one more task.
A relapse draped in lingerie,
A curse you beg to never sway.

But still we chase, despite the cost,
For in his fire, we feel less lost.
You voiced the ache, the pull, the lie,
The kind you crave, though it will fry.

So here I stand, your mirrored shade,
A victim too of games he played.
Poet to poet, I confess
Your pain, your truth I must profess

It is art that bleeds with savage grace,
A love too raw for time to erase.
So, write again, I'll read it deep,
For some confessions help us sleep

Even if the dream's too steep.

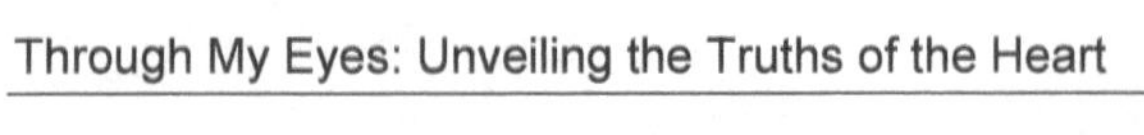

James 1:14–15 (KJV)

"But every man is tempted, when he is drawn away of his own lust, and enticed. Then when lust hath conceived, it bringeth forth sin: and sin, when it is finished, bringeth forth death."

"From Shadows to Light"

I don't belong with men who fear
The dreams I chase, the truths I clear.
My voice is loud, my stance is bold,
My worth is fire, not bought or sold.

I'm not ashamed of what I seek,
A life of love, not cold or weak.
I won't just dream I plan, pursue,
And build a life both deep and true.

I crave a bond, not games or doubt,
Where love is shown and talked about.
A partner proud to walk beside,
Not one who hides or runs to hide.

Let's walk in daylight, hand in hand,
Not shadows where I barely stand.
I long for talks that make me feel,
Not guessing games, but something real.

I love the laughter of our kids,
The zoo, the park, the joy that lives.
But why the "no," the constant flake?
When family calls, why must hearts break?

I want to feel not just pretend
That love won't pause, that joy won't end.
I need a man who dreams out loud,
Who stands with me, both strong and proud.

"Hey love, what do you think?" he'll say,
And build with me a brighter way.
Not Superman, but kind and true,
Who fits my soul in all we do.

Each sleepless night, I call in prayer,
"Dear Lord, please send him if he's there."
Not one who fakes or acts the part,
But one who sees and guards my heart.

I'm not weak for wanting more
I've learned what love is truly for.
This ache, this tear, this deep unrest,
Is truth emerging from my chest.

I'm grieving dreams that won't come true,
Because they weren't meant for me and you.
But this is growth, a rising flame,
From hopeful tears, I stake my claim.

I seek connection, joy, and grace,
Not cold confusion I must chase.
The man who matches heart and mind,
Who's not afraid of what he'll find.

He'll love my voice, not try to hush,
He'll match my steps, not make me rush.
He'll dream with me, we'll plan, we'll grow,
In open light, not gloom or woe.

So, hear me now, O sky above,
Align my path with honest love.
I'm done with guessing, games, and pain,
I want the sun not to storm and rain.

The one who walks with God and me,
Will speak my name and set me free.
No more shadows, no disguise
Just love that meets me eye to eye.

This isn't fantasy or flair,
It's what my soul was made to bear.
I'm not too much I'm just enough,
I'm fierce, I'm whole, I'm strong, I'm tough.

So let me rise, and close this door,
To lesser love I'll crave no more.
He's not the one and that's alright
The real one walks in love and light

1 John 1:7 (KJV)

"But if we walk in the light, as he is in the light, we have fellowship one with another, and the blood of Jesus Christ his Son cleanseth us from all sin."

"The Man Who Vanished in My Light"

He used to say, "Let's go, my love," then smile and take my hand,
Now silence greets my triumphs he no longer makes a stand.
Three days later, he comes and goes, with stories worn and thin,
I searched his eyes for answers, but there's no truth within.

He once would call me partner, now he leaves me in the shade,
No "Let's go celebrate," just ghosts of joy we made.
He runs his errands all alone, like I was never there,
And I'm left holding questions wrapped in cold and empty air.

Is this the man who held my dreams and swore he'd hold me down?
Or someone scared of how I shine, afraid he'll lose his crown?
I begged for love that doesn't flinch when I begin to rise,
Not love that hides behind a mask and comforts me with lies.

I don't need grand illusions or a lover dressed in fear,
I need someone who stays close when my breakthroughs draw near.
Someone who claps when I succeed, not walks the other way,
Who doesn't leave me guessing at the end of every day.

You vanish when I need you most what does that even mean?
Real love won't shrink or disappear just cause the light turns green.
I want a friend, a soul unashamed, who'd proudly call me "mine,"
Not someone who retreats in shadows every time I shine.

So, call it what truly is emotional neglect,
A partner's job is not to leave your heart a wreck.
I won't keep dancing in the dark while you slip out the door,
I've got no space for fake love now I won't pretend no more.

You taught me something painful, but I'm wiser from the fall,
I'll build a life of real love now no begging, none.
So, when the truth is hard to face, remember what is right:
A real one shows up stronger when you step into your light.

Proverbs 4:18 (KJV)

"But the path of the just is as the shining light, that shineth more and more unto the perfect day."

"Dream On"

You are the wish in a silent prayer,
The whispered hope in midnight air.
A treasure rare, a soul so true
You are someone's dream come true.

Let no one dim your brilliant light,
Or steal your stars in dead of night.
For hearts that stall or fail to see,
Are not the ones for destiny.

So, if they linger, lost and gone,
Wasting time just dreams on.
You're not a stop on someone's way
You are the reason hearts should stay

Psalm 37:4 (KJV)

"Delight thyself also in the Lord; and he shall give thee the desires of thine heart."
A beautiful promise for someone who's still waiting but *refuses to settle.*

"Say It Softly If You Care"

You say you want to lift me high,
To be my strength when spirits cry.
You say you're here to ease my pain,
But speak in thunder, not in rain.

Your words, they try to build a bridge,
But trembles near the edge's ridge.
You ask me how to let you in,
Yet wear a mask too thick, too thin.

Support, my love, is not a shout,
It's holding space when I'm in doubt.
It's quiet eyes and open hands,
Not rushed demands or harsh commands.

If love is real, let it be still,
Not charged with guilt or forceful will.
I need to breathe, not brace my chest,
To feel calm, not take a test.

It's not that you don't care at all
It's that your tone builds up a wall.
So, if you truly want to know,
Don't rush me just to ease your woe.

Support is not a race to win,
It's patience from the soul, within.
It's asking me, then letting be,
Not turning all the light to thee.

So, hold your heart, and let me share,
Say it softly if you care.
Then I can open, then I'll trust,
In love that's safe, and kind, and just.

1 Corinthians 13:4–5 (KJV)

"Charity suffereth long, and is kind… seeketh not her own, is not easily provoked, thinketh no evil."

"Speak to Me in Truth"

Thank you for the words you shared,
The way you showed how much you cared.
Your love for me was loud and clear,
And in your praise, I felt you near.

You saw me fighting through the pain,
Through pouring tears and heavy rain.
You saw me stand when it got tough,
You called my love more than enough.

But love, there's something I must say,
A truth I can't just brush away.
Not out of spite, not out of pride
But to keep trust from slipping wide.

That message meant the world to me,
But why not send it privately?
In front of him, my child's own dad,
A line was crossed, and it felt sad.

Not because I doubt the heart you hold,
But cause our bond is quite gold.
The kind of love that grows in shade,
Not on display, not loudly made.

I know you've battled ghosts before,
That still knocks softly at your door.
Abandonment, it carved its mark,
It left you reaching in the dark.

And still, you love with all your soul,
But fear can sometimes take control.
You share to prove you have a place,
But love, you never need that race.

I see your heart, I feel your fight,
I know you long to make things right.
But let us build in sacred space,

Not through a screen, but face to face.

Let's write our love with steady pen,
Not shaken hands, or "what if" when.
Let trust be stronger than the scars,
And meet each other where we are.

So, thank you for the things you said,
The way you lift me when I'm dead.
But speak to me in truth and grace
Let's keep our love in its right place.

Not for the world, not for their eyes
But where real love and healing rise.

Proverbs 25:11 (KJV)

"A word fitly spoken is like apples of gold in pictures of silver."

"You Matter"

They took her things, they mocked her name,
They laughed and pointed, played their game.
She sat alone, her voice so small,
No one heard her silent call.

A ChapStick gone, a pencil thrown,
A heart that felt so much alone.
Assigned a seat, then pushed aside,
She wore a brave face, but still she cried.

They told her that she cried too loud,
Too soft, too weird, not made too crowded.
She rolled and fell, no hand was near,
Just aching bones and silent fear.

She told the grownups what they had been,
But still it hurt beneath her skin.
A voice inside began to lie,
"You're not enough, so say goodbye."

But that voice isn't heaven sent,
It's not from light, it's not content.
It whispers hate, it breeds the pain,
It tells you lies to twist your brain.

The truth is love, the truth is grace,
The truth is found in warm embrace.
You're made for more than they believe,
You plant bright seeds they can't conceive.

A parent's tear, a father's plea
"You're here on Earth for destiny.
When life gives lemons, make them sweet,
Stand tall with hope upon your feet."

"Your story's yours, don't hand it out,
To those who laugh, or those who doubt.
You are not here to fade or bend,
Your life's a light someone will mend."

So, if you're hurting, know this true
You're not alone, someone loves you.
And when that voice comes creeping nearby,
Say, "I am strong. I will stay here."

Let music lift, let kindness grow,
Let all the pain you feel be known.
For every heart that's ever bled,
Deserves to rise, not hang its head.

So, take this poem, wear it proud,
Say every word out clear and loud
"I matter here; I'm not a ghost.
I may be quiet, but I'm needed most."

Psalm 139:14 (KJV)

"I will praise thee; for I am fearfully and wonderfully made marvellous are thy works; and that my soul knoweth right well."

"Listen to the Voice"

Some kids at school keep picking fights,
Steals my stuff, then laughs in spite.
Took my seat, my snacks, my space,
Like I don't belong in this whole place.

Friends that smiled now turn away,
Say I'm "too much" or cry all day.
Whispers pass from ear to ear,
Till secrets sting and friendships smear.

They said I'm loud, said I'm a mess,
Just because I hurt and tried to express myself.
And when I fell down from the stands,
No one rushed with helping hands.

I told the teacher I was brave
But I felt ignored like I should cave.
One kind soul just stopped and said,
"What's going on inside your head?"

She asked me why I felt so low,
I tried to speak, let pieces show.
She sent me back to class again,
But still I felt I had no friends.

Then music came and brought some light,
My favorite teacher shined so brightly.
Her voice, a song, a peaceful sound,
The only time I felt unbound.

But then the call broke the air.
They told my mom I didn't care.
That I had said I'd end it all,
Because of pain, it's too big, too tall.

My mother cried and gripped my hand,
Said, "That's not part of God's own plan.
You don't decide when life should end,

You're here to grow, to heal, to mend."

My father's voice came deep and strong,
"You're here for purpose, not for wrong.
The devil lies inside your head
God's truth brings love and peace instead."

He said, "You're smart, you're brave, you shine,
You're made from light, you're God's design.
You're not a burden, not a ghost,
You matter here. You matter most."

"When life gives lemons, find the sweet,
Stand tall again on steady feet.
Those friends who left were never true,
They were a storm just passing through."

"So, write your story, own each page,
Let strength and joy replace the rage.
Don't live for them, live loud, live free,
This world still needs the gift of me."

So now I fight the voice of lies,
And listen to the One who tries
To lift me up when I feel small,
To say I am enough, through all.

I matter now, I matter still,
I have a heart; I have a will.
So, if you hear a voice so cold
That's not the truth you need to hold.

The voice of truth says, "You belong."
It sings inside you, deep and strong.
So, breathe, stand up, and make some noise

You're loved. You're light. Now listen to the Voice.

Jeremiah 29:11 (KJV)

"For I know the thoughts that I think toward you, saith the Lord, thoughts of peace, and not of evil, to give you an expected end."

"The Slam of Morning"

This morning cracked like thunder's cry,
A storm behind each door swung high.
No words, no kisses, no soft goodbye,
Just echoes where your love should lie.

The hallway groaned beneath your tread,
As if you marched through thoughts unsaid.
The baby slept, our peace was spread
You stirred the still, you woke the dead.

The Google speaker, loud and proud,
Declared your mood without a sound.
Its booming voice, a shrouded shroud
You made the silence feel too loud.

You used to hum or plug your ears,
To spare the house your morning gears.
But now it's slams and passive sneers,
Like noise could fix what took you years.

You closed my door, you cracked her wide,
As if to say, "She's on my side."
But in that hush, I heard the tide
Of something cold you try to hide.

You skipped my room, skipped my face,
You used your leaving to displace
The warmth, the calm, the soft embrace
You turned our home into a race.

A race to wake, to rattle, jar,
To bruise without the visible scar.
No fight, no flare, no open spar
Just wounds that whisper what you are.

Yet I still ask, beneath the din,
What war you waged, what hurt within?
What silent grief did not begin
Until the slamming let it in?

This isn't how we greet the day,
Not with your love so far away.
If pain is knocking let it stay.
But speak, not slam, to have your say.

Ephesians 4:31–32 (KJV)

"Let all bitterness, and wrath, and anger, and clamour, and evil speaking, be put away from you, with all malice:
And be ye kind one to another, tenderhearted, forgiving one another, even as God for Christ's sake hath forgiven you."

"To the Warrior Mother"

To the mother who wakes with tears in her eyes,
Still facing the day neath unwelcoming skies,
Who carries the weight though her spirit feels sore,
And gives from a heart that can't give anymore.

To the queen in the kitchen with nothing but scraps,
Yet turns them to feasts in her magical laps,
Whoever hums through the hunger, hides every bruise,
And still finds a way to love and to choose.

To the mother abandoned, left torn and betrayed,
Whose partner walked out, but she stayed unafraid,
She looked in at her children and saw the divine,
And vowed they'd be whole, come rainstorm or shine.

To the soul who once cradled a child now gone,
Yet still finds the strength to keep living on,
She smiles through memories, broken but brave,
Planting hope like wildflowers over their grave.

To the mother who lies by a man full of lies,
Who steals with his silence, who cheats with his eyes,
But she stands for her babies, a fortress of grace,
Wearing heartbreak and hope on the same weary face.

To the mother unseen in a world moving fast,
Who's saving her children while stuck in the past,
Fighting off bullies, both grown and unkind,
A shield made of fire, of body and mind.

To the mothers who ache but still hold the line,
Who laughs through their sorrow, pretending they're fine,
This poem is your mirror, your truth, and your light
You're the soul of the stars in the darkest night.

For your grace under fire, your fierce, sacred tears,
Your wisdom that's deeper than countless old years,
For loving when loveless, for holding on tight,

You're the warrior mother, the flame in the night.
May this day be your anthem, your healing, your song,
You've carried the burden, so heavy, so long.
Now I hear this, dear sister, so noble, so true
The whole world is brighter because it has you.

Proverbs 31:25–26 (KJV)

*"Strength and honour are her clothing; and she shall rejoice in time to come.
She openeth her mouth with wisdom; and in her tongue is the law of kindness."*

"Secret Screens and Morning Scenes"

I rise and shine, the morning's glow,
But something's off deep down, I know.
He's on his phone, all quiet, sly,
No "good morning," just a quick goodbye.

I stir, he shifts, puts it away,
Then holds my hands in a clumsy way.
He's never one to hug in bed,
But now he's kissing my sleepy head.

His arms around me, snug and tight,
But why the show at morning light?
That sudden warmth, that fake cares
Feels more like guilt than tenderness.

I'm not a fool, I feel the shade,
In secret swipes and games, he's played.
His phone, his world I'm locked outside,
And in that space, the truth can hide.

I want a love that's bold and true,
Not midnight texts I never knew.
I won't pretend, I see the signs,
Of hidden paths and crossed up lines.

I won't grow old with secret schemes,
Or be a ghost inside his dreams.
If he won't open his life,
He's not the man to call me "wife."

So, rise and shine, I've seen the light
No love should bloom in shadowed night.
The truth is clear, I won't be blind,
I need a heart that's not confined.

Luke 8:17 (KJV)

*"For nothing is secret, that shall not be made manifest;
neither anything hid, that shall not be known and come abroad."*

"The Secret Hour"

I woke at dawn, the light was thin,
My partner's face wore a quiet sin.
His fingers danced on glowing screen,
Then vanished quickly like no one was seen.

He reached for me, all soft and sly,
A hug he never gives oh why?
That sudden warmth, it didn't fit,
A gesture born from guilt, not grit.

The silence screamed, it told the tale,
Of hidden truths behind the veil.
His eyes were shut, but I could see
He's living life apart from me.

A secret world he thinks unknown,
While I lie waking, cold, alone.
My heart knows when things feel strange,
It feels like the shift, the quiet change.

I've felt it near my dearest friend,
His mother doesn't end.
The walls go up, I'm left outside,
While he retreats, I swallow pride.

I'm not at peace, I'm not held tight,
I'm not embraced in morning light.
Not seen, not heard, not loved out loud
Just buried in his silent shroud.

A man who loves should not conceal,
Should not make touch a way to heal
The wound he caused just moments passed,
Then hide again, as if it's cast.

I crave a bond that's clear and free,
Not cryptic love or mystery.
I should not need to play the sleuth,
To claw my way to reach the truth.

The sacred space of love's domain
Can't thrive on secrets, lies, or strain.
If hearts can't meet with open grace,
Then I must leave this haunted place.

For trust is not a game of chance,
Nor is love built on sly advance.
My soul cries out it knows the cost
In loving him, too much is lost.

So, I will rise, reclaim my fire,
Realign my heart, my soul, desire.
Let peace return where pain once stood,
And walk away for my own good.

I'm not a fool, I'm not confused,
I won't be hidden or misused.
Love doesn't leave you feeling small
I choose myself, and that says all.

Proverbs 12:22 (KJV)

*"Lying lips are abomination to the Lord:
but they that deal truly are his delight."*

"While You Lecture, I Chase"

Your best friend's words still echo clear,
Like I'm not enough just standing here.
She says if she were near, she'd stay
She'd come to class and sit all day.

She'd hold your hand and watch you teach,
Like love was simple, in easy reach.
But words are cheap when life is free,
No kids, no ties, no cries like me.

No lunches packed with sleepy eyes,
No park runs under heavy skies.
No searching for a sitter late,
No juggling life with hands full of fate.

You tell me what I could have done,
Like I had options, like this is fun.
But while you climbed, I held the base,
Built the life, then lost my place.

You knew the path, you knew the strain
What we'd lose, and what you'd gain.
And still you watched me fall behind,
While praising her "supportive" mind.

But I see more than you can grasp,
I see through words, behind the mask.
What she gives you is light and air,
What I give is always there.

So now you ask me to attend,
To play the role she would pretend.
But I'm not her, I can't just glide,
With a toddler yelling at my side.

I walked into your world today,
But I don't walk in all the way.
I chase our child, balloon in hand,

While you just talk, they call it "grand."

He runs and climbs, I chase and bend,
No one sees what I defend.
He's up the stairs, he's through the door,
I'm running circles on the floor.

I try to focus, try to stay,
But I'm just orbiting your day.
You say she could support you more,
But she's not the one you swore before.

She has no ties, no sleepless nights,
No spilled juice or potty fights.
She has the time to watch you speak
I have a life that doesn't peak.

And here I am, unseen again,
Invisible among your friends.
She gets applause for just a smile,
I get ignored after each mile.

So, stop comparing what we give,
Stop pretending this is how we live.
She may be more to you right now,
But I'm the one who made that vow.

And while you talk, I walk through these halls,
With sticky hands and echoed calls.
Two hours straight, I pace alone,
While you feel seen and in your zone.

All because a "friend" got praise,
And I got blame for tougher days.
But this is loving the real, the raw
The kind that aches beneath the flaw.

So next time you stand and speak so proudly,
Remember me behind the crowd.
Not just the mother, not just your mate,
But the soul who still carries your fate.

Proverbs 31:27–28 (KJV)

*"She looketh well to the ways of her household,
and eateth not the bread of idleness.
Her children arise up, and call her blessed;
her husband also, and he praiseth her."*

"Awakening in the Silence"

I stood in the shadow of all we once knew,
Where laughter grew quiet, and colors withdrew.
I whispered to memories, soft in my mind,
But I found only echoes, no peace left to find.

The past came to visit, unwelcomed, unkind,
A ghost in our bed, in the back of your mind.
You're holding a love that was never my name,
And I stood in the cold while you fed the flame.

Is it me who is drifting or you who stood still?
Have I run out of heart, or just out of will?
You paused our forever to carry your pain,
And I waited in silence, through heartbreak and rain.

I wanted a love that could shelter and speak,
Not silence and secrets week after week.
You held back your truth like a bird in a cage,
While I softened my soul and swallowed my rage.

I dreamed of a partner, a life with no fear,
Now I question if you were ever truly here.
I asked for assurance, for trust without doubt,
But the more that I begged, the more I burned out.

I've tried and I've given, I've knelt and I've prayed,
Now I look at the wreckage of love we both made.
I picture another, a life warm and wide,
And wonder if peace might live on that side.

Am I wrong to let go? Have I drifted too far?
Or was I always alone, just chasing your star?
Emotionally numb, yet heavy with grace,
I've lost you and found me in the very same place.

A therapist sees me now clear through the pain,
A soul seeking safety again and again.
A coach says to rise, to reclaim what I need,
To plant a new garden, not water old seed.

A psychologist names it: my mind's breaking free,
From loops of old longing and lost fantasy.
And Spirit reminds me: this ache is the key
To walk through the fire and finally be me.

So, this is awakening, quiet but loud,
Not a scream in the dark, but a stand in the crowd.
Not drifting, but rising, though weary and worn
Not broken by love just ready to be reborn.

Isaiah 43:18–19 (KJV)

*"Remember ye not the former things,
neither consider the things of old.
Behold, I will do a new thing;
now it shall spring forth; shall ye not know it?
I will even make a way in the wilderness,
and rivers in the desert."*

"Still in Here"

I'm thinking of you again tonight,
The stars are dim, but your memories are bright.
The letters we wrote, the ink now dry,
Still whisper truths we can't deny.

You gave me a chance, then drifted away,
Too far to hold yet close each day.
I felt the break when you left our place,
A silent tear ran down my face.

I knew you'd go, I felt it then,
We'd never be as we had been.
We said goodbye with quiet grace,
But time can't seem to fill your space.

You can't come near, and we both know why,
We'd lose ground, no need to try.
We'd fall again, too deep, too fast
Some loves are never meant to last.

The care you gave, the shield, the flame,
It faded, but I feel the same.
You're far, I know, but in my soul,
Your echoes still refuse control.

The nights we stayed up past the moon,
The tree you waited for at noon,
The breakfast shared with you and your dad
All moments that I wish I had.

The past is old, but sharp and near,
It whispers loud when you're not here.
Though time moves on and seasons flee,
Your heart still beats inside of me.

So, if I smile or seem just fine,
I knew half this heart was always thin.
The memories stay; they won't let go
Their roots are too deep to ever show.

Ecclesiastes 3:1, 6b (KJV)

*"To everything there is a season,
and a time to every purpose under the heaven:
...a time to keep, and a time to cast away."*

"The End of gaslighting, The Beginning of Peace"

There is no confusion here.
I saw what I saw.
I felt what I felt.
The truth doesn't bend itself to comfort denial,
and I won't waste my light debating shadows anymore.

I gave love. I gave chances. I stood in honesty,
even when it cost me pieces of my peace.
But I will not be gaslit into blindness
My eyes were open. My heart knew.
And I trust that knowing now more than ever.

I deserve clarity, not chaos.
Truth not twisted silence.
Sacred honesty not spiritual spin.

So, I release you, fully.
Go live your truth, however it fits you.
But stop trying to edit mine.

I'm choosing peace over proving.
I'm walking forward and I'm not looking back.

Isaiah 26:3 (KJV)

"Thou wilt keep him in perfect peace, whose mind is stayed on thee: because he trusteth in thee."

"Let Me Be, Let Truth Be Seen"

Why would you settle to live in the shade,
A whisper, a secret, a choice that you made.
You know who I am don't act so small,
Show your whole face, or don't show at all.

Don't spare my feelings with cowardly pride,
Don't think I don't see what you try to hide.
I walk down the stairs, the line goes dead
You're worth more than silence and words unsaid.

He hangs up quickly like I shouldn't hear,
But I see the picture, it's perfectly clear.
I'm not even mad, I'm already gone,
He's been stringing you both, playing wrong with us.

He showed me for years that love wasn't real,
So why should I care what he tries to conceal?
There's no more beef, I gave him to you
I'm just left wondering: who are you too?

You don't have to hide, or play pretend,
You both could be honest, this doesn't have to bend.
Tell him to let me go I'll walk away,
So y'all can step into light, not lie each day.

He weaponizes God to make me stay,
But God don't live in lies and games he plays.
He calls you then hangs up like I don't know,
That speaks enough the truth will show.

The price he's paying you must be steep,
To be a secret he's working to keep.
But go on, be with him, you've got the green light
I won't be hidden; I won't dim my light.

He says "we" and drags me to therapy too,
But the only one healing is likely you.

He makes me question the things I see,
When all I've asked for is honesty.

I held him down, never broke a vow,
I don't want him to have him now.
When we're with family or playing with kids,
He sneaks off to talk, that's what he did.

I want a love that's open and true,
Not toxic or secret, not masked in blue.
He breaks me down to make me leave,
So, he won't have to face the web he weaves.

Two hearts he's lying to, twisting the thread,
That's why we'll never get to wed.
He whispers to you, "If she comes, hang up,"
But baby, that's not love that's a poisoned cup.

I pray the next soul he finds sees clear,
That they know God and draw Him near.
May couples' therapy helps him grow,
Because I'm done helping, I've let him go.

Maybe the next one won't be strong like me,
They'll need him healed, not hurting endlessly.
He tried to gaslight, confuse, and lie,
But I see through the script I don't ask why.

He said he's "stumped," that there's no scheme,
But confusion's his cover, not what it seems.
He's "perplexed" and "babe," but I see the spin,
He's just scared cause I won't give in.

This isn't love, it's control and fear,
But I choose light, I'm getting clear.
You can have him, take his lies too
I'm building a life that's honest and true.

So go be his secret if that's what you need,
But I'll be the woman who chose to be freed.
No more shadows, no silent screams
I walk in truth. I walk in dreams.

Ephesians 5:11 (KJV)

"And have no fellowship with the unfruitful works of darkness, but rather reprove them."

"Today Was a Special Day"

Today was a special day for me,
A dream unveiled for all to see.
My book released, my voice set free,
Yet shadows danced where light should be.

He mowed the lawn, phone at his ear,
A whisper cloaked in hidden fear.
A thread deleted, secrets tight,
He masked his truth and veiled the light.

He sat across the couch just right,
So, I'd descend and miss the sight.
But I came down, and caught the tone
He whispered low, but not alone.

A name unspoken, soft goodbyes,
He looked away, avoided eyes.
Why hide a call, why choose disguise?
When love is true, it never lies.

For three long years, this dance, this game,
The stress, the hurt, the quiet shame.
I begged for truth; he blamed me
Then made my tears about his pain.

But I've grown strong, I've found my way,
I journal now; I seize my day.
I honor peace, I don't pretend,
I see the signs that never end.

A partner shares, a partner shows,
Not secrets kept in whispered throes.
He talks of me to someone new
But not in light, just shaded hue.

What kind of love must hide its face,
Or vanish without leaving trace?
Why must a name stay locked away,
On such a bright and sacred day?

Perhaps an ex, a job, a friend,
Or someone else he must defend.
But one truth clear, through all he hides
His loyalty no longer rides.

So, this I claim, and say out loud
I will not live beneath this cloud.
I deserve joy, not silent cries,
A love that holds no need for lies.

Today was special mine to own.
A day of truth, and how I've grown.
And though his shadow tried to play
I shine too bright to fade away.

Luke 8:17 (KJV)

"For nothing is secret, that shall not be made manifest; neither any thing hid, that shall not be known and come abroad."

"Admired in Words, Abandoned in Truth"

You say you admire me, call me divine,
But your voice turns sharp, crosses every line.
You praise with your lips, but your actions betray,
In shadows and secrets, you slip far away.

You yell, you accuse, you twist what I see,
Then ask why I'm broken when you're hurting me.
You lie to my face with a sweet smile,
Then damage my mind till I feel defeated.

You whisper with others, you hide and deceive,
And I still expect to trust and believe.
You call me by names not meant for my soul,
Then act like it's love while losing control.

A mirror you hold with a shattered face,
Reflecting on a world where I'm out of place.
You gift me confusion, wrapped up in charm,
But none of it shields me from ongoing harm.

A therapist might say, "This is control,"
A war on the mind that's taking its toll.
It's gaslighting, darling emotional theft,
Stealing your truth till there's nothing left.

A spiritual guide would look at your pain,
Say his wounds speak loud through actions insane.
But pain's no excuse for a spirit to bleed,
You deserve light, not a garden of need.

Both would agree, and I now can too:
True love doesn't damage the heart it clings to.
Respect isn't shouted or buried in lies,
It's shown in the truth that never denies.

So, I rise from the fog, reclaiming my name,
Refusing to dance in a two-faced game.
For I am not here to be broken or used

Admired in words, but in spirit abused.

Psalm 34:18 (KJV)

"The Lord is nigh unto them that are of a broken heart; and saveth such as be of a contrite spirit."

"The Eyes That Wander, the Soul That Sleeps"

Their gaze, automatic, like breath in the night,
No thought behind it, no inner sight.
A flicker, a glance, not measured or planned,
But born of a mind they don't understand.

They seek stimulation, a thrill in disguise,
Or chase validation through wandering eyes.
Subconscious perhaps, yet bold and clear,
A signal that something is missing here.

When it's constant and loud, like a siren's cry,
It chips at your worth and questions why.
Is it power they seek to pull you down low?
To test your heart with a quiet blow?

It may not be malice, but distance instead,
A symptom of feelings long left unsaid.
Dissatisfaction behind the façade,
A silent retreat from emotional Guide.

Yet hurt doesn't wait for an explanation,
Nor rest in the arms of rationalization.
You feel what you feel deep, unrefined
And pain doesn't pause to see what's behind.

They may not know it stings like a dart,
Or understand how it fractures the heart.
If their world once called it normal and fine,
That history still doesn't justify the line.

Respect isn't shaped by culture alone,
It's learned when we care, when love is shown.
So, speak from your truth, don't dim your flame,
You're not too much you're not to blame.

For love that is blind to the wounds it brings,
It is love that forgets the weight of small things.
And eyes that wander without a clue,

Can lose the soul that once saw you

Proverbs 4:25-27 (KJV):

*"Let thine eyes look right on, and let thine eyelids look straight before thee.
Ponder the path of thy feet, and let all thy ways be established.
Turn not to the right hand nor to the left: remove thy foot from evil."*

"When Love Stops Speaking"

Why are you cheering for my bright debut,
Yet silent when I need something true?
You clap for my wins, so loud and so proud,
But when I cry softly, you are lost in the crowd.

Two days you vanished, no word, no invite,
Just went to the store and stayed out past night.
Then day three you left, took our precious one to,
No "Would you like to come?" just goodbye.

You once told me stories of work and the strain,
Now silence has swallowed the mundane.
You wait till I ask, then speak in a blur
Your eyes never quit where they were.

From a mind trained to clinically see,
This shift smells of emotional absentee.
You lift my win to avoid looking in,
Fearing the storm, you hold deep within.

Withdrawing from things we once would do,
Is your quiet rebellion,
Maybe resentment has taken the floor,
Or you're aching inside and closing the door.

Relationship wisdom has more to unfold
My rise may leave you feeling less bold.
You may not know how to sit with my soul,
So instead, you drift, losing control.

Not all were raised to hold love with grace
Some flee from emotion, from eye-to-eye space.
You may feel I press while I simply confide,
But pressure to you is just me by your side.

Spiritually speaking, I'm rising each day,
While you, perhaps, have chosen to stay.
I'm walking in purpose, I'm shedding my skin

You stay at the threshold, too scared to walk in.
My win is my healing, my grief on the page,
And you're stuck in silence, entrapped by your cage.
I'm not your mirror, I'm more than your past
And maybe that truth is too heavy to grasp.

I'm not too much I'm clear, awake.
This ache in my soul? It's not a mistake.
It's the voice of my spirit saying, "You've grown."
And maybe it's time I walk alone.

But first comes the talk, the soul-to-soul call
To say what I feel, to risk it all.
To ask "Will you meet me, heart open and wide?
Or stay in the shadows where love goes to hide?"

If you won't rise, then I must still soar
For silence like yours I'll carry no more.
I'm not asking too much. I'm asking for me
To be loved with depth, and to finally be free.

Amos 3:3 (KJV)

"Can two walk together, except they be agreed?"

"Not Self-Destruction"

It's not self-destruction, I'm fighting to breathe,
I don't want to go back, but I can't truly leave.
Trapped in a cycle, no ride, no release,
No jobs in the silence, no hint of peace.

Tumbled through shadows, fell out of grace,
Independence vanished without a trace.
No will to remain in a place so grim,
A crash hit hard, was it her or him?

You act like you know, but your guess is blind,
You don't see the scars etched deep in my mind.
Regret like a weight, and debt like a chain,
But I won't bow down, I'll fight through the pain.

Each morning, I rise, I reach for the light,
I dream of escaping, I prepare for the flight.
This isn't seduction, no curse I impose,
Just a life washed clean, where peace softly grows.

No games, no lies, no secrets to keep,
Just trust and protection in love runs deep.
Loyal and strong, with joy in my chest,
A heart full of grace, a soul truly blessed.

I lost who I was, my purpose, my name,
But I walk with Christ, through fire and flame.
Intentions were pure, my hopes soared high,
I just feared the truth and the tears in my eyes.

But still I move forward, one step, then more,
Toward a life that's better than ever before.
It's not self-destruction it's strength in disguise,
It's a storm I'll conquer, with fire in my eyes.

2 Corinthians 4:8-9 (KJV)

"We are troubled on every side, yet not distressed; we are perplexed, but not in despair; Persecuted, but not forsaken; cast down, but not destroyed."

"I Noticed You Didn't Reply When I Shared My Breakup"

I noticed your silence, it cut like a blade,
When I reached out in heartbreak, alone and afraid.
You vanished, no echo, not even a sigh,
From someone I trusted and now I ask why.

Was there more underneath that I didn't yet, see?
Something with my partner, kept hidden from me?
I searched through the quiet, confused by the lack,
Of care in your words, or the warmth I thought back.

You came to the play, but not to my pain,
That moment was sunny but soaked in the rain.
Your presence in public, yet absence in soul,
Left questions and ache in a heart full of holes.

I don't want the mask, the polite little nod,
I'm not here for theater or faking applaud.
I'm asking for truth not silence or show,
If something is broken, I need to know.

So please, no illusions, no dancing around,
No smiles in the spotlight while truth's underground.
I'm reaching it again, though it's hard to be bold
But I won't chase answers in stories half told.

Proverbs 27:6 (KJV)

"Faithful are the wounds of a friend; but the kisses of an enemy are deceitful."

"Mirror in the Shadow"

It's the strangest thing I can't explain,
A tug at my heart, a whisper of pain.
At an event, all dressed in light,
I spoke with someone, bold and bright.

A woman of rank, with wisdom and grace,
While you stood watching, lost in my space.
Eyes not on our precious one, not on the scene,
But on my words sharp, focused, keen.

A voice close whispered, soft and low,
You're chasing my light wherever you go."
Didn't even glance at the precious one we share,
As if I was the only one standing there.

Today again, the past returned,
Another strange moment, my spirit burned.
I left our precious one with love and trust,
In the backyard air, as all parents must.

My hands were busy, cleaning the floor,
But you kept coming in and out the door.
Backyard, front yard, windows ajar
Eyes like questions, watching from afar.

Not once, but thrice, this rhythm plays,
You checks on me in curious ways.
At your kins house, across the room,
When "wedding?" was asked, he crossed the gloom.

He stood beside, not to speak or share,
But just to breathe my very air.
Now you copy what I do and say,
Like I'm the sun, and you're my day.

I grab a snack, you grabs one too,
I vibe alone; you copy the view.
"I like the way you're chillin' there,"
You say, then follows, unaware.

It's not just mimic it's something more,
Like you are trapped outside your own soul door.
Like you need my vibe to find your pace,
But forget we've got a precious one to ease.

From the mind
It feels like you're trying to make amends
Not for wrongs, but for your own sense,
Placing your peace upon my shelf.

Emotional lines are deeply blurred,
Love that's unbalanced, unsaid, unheard.
As if you fear to stand alone,
You're seeking my steps to find your own.

It could be attachment, lost in a haze.
Mirroring, watching, unsure how to behave,
So, you just reflect what you see in me.

But it's a pull too deep, a silent cry.
A bond too heavy, energy drained,
Your presence too close, my spirit strained.

This isn't balance not this way.
Relationships means we both must lead,
Not one to follow, and one to bleed.

Where is support, the equal stance?
Where is the rhythm, the mutual dance?
I carry the child, the chores, the weight
While you just orbit, calling it fate.

Territorial moves he cannot hide.
Body mimics, watching eyes
Longing worn as a poor disguise.

I move, you copy, watches still,
More of a shadow than a will.
Not malicious, but unclear,
Rooted in love, perhaps, but fear.

I ask Jesus my father above,
What does this all reflect in me?
Why do I feel so unseen,
With someone who's always on the scene?

This isn't malice, but it's not quite love,
It lacks the ground, the hand, the shove
The shared push through parent days,
The silent strength in mundane ways.

So here I am, confused but wise,
With open heart and sharpened eyes.
I seek a bond that builds, not clings,
Not just the echo of my wings.

I'll let you stand and find your voice,
To love by will, and not by choice.
For love is not a mirrored face,
It's two whole souls in a sacred place.

Proverbs 25:19 (KJV)

"Confidence in an unfaithful man in time of trouble is like a broken tooth, and a foot out of joint."

"My Partner's Time, My Summer's Cry"

My partner's off work, but we're not on the go,
No bags to be packed, no places to show.
He's home on the couch, just resting his head,
While dreams of our summer lay quietly dead.

A break, I get that we all need to breathe,
But then comes another with nothing beneath.
Two more days vanished like wind through the trees,
While I'm left here juggling plans on my knees.

Is it on purpose? I don't really know,
But our time's shrinking, it's painfully slow.
We talked about vacations, laughter and sand,
Yet he takes his time solo, was this what we planned?

Perhaps he's burned out, too weary to speak,
Or lost in a silence that's heavy and bleak.
Is this escape or just something deeper?
A retreat from the noise, a craving for sleep?

If he would just tell me what's going on,
We might build a summer before it is gone.
But now I feel stranded, unheard and alone,
While he carves out peace in a house that's our own.

I don't think it's cruel, or done out of spite,
But the shadow it casts blocks our family's light.
If only he'd see what these choices can cost

The warmth of a season, the moments we've lost.
So, I'll try to speak calmly, with heart open wide,
To reach past the silence he keeps deep inside.
We can't find a rhythm unless we both play
And I want us dancing through bright summer days.

Ecclesiastes 3:1 (KJV)

"To every thing there is a season, and a time to every purpose under the heaven:"

"The Pause Between the Lines"

He asked, "Just hold, I've got a call,"
You nodded, knowing work meant all.
You gave him space, you let him be,
Respecting time and boundaries free.

But when he came back, something changed,
Your voice, though calm, was slightly strained.
You asked, "That call what was it for?"
But laced with tone that questioned more.

He blinked, then paused, said, "Huh?" again,
His voice was soft, unlike back then.
A fidget here, a glance away,
His calm had seemed to slip astray.

The words came slow, like pulled from mist,
As if the truth had met a twist.
A guilty twitch, a nervous laugh,
As though he walked a shadowed path.

Was it the tone that made him freeze?
Or secrets blowing in the breeze?
A lie perhaps he tried to build,
While silence in the room was filled.

He might have felt caught in a snare,
The weight of judgment in the air.
Or maybe truth just wouldn't flow,
Unsure of how much you should know.

So now you're left to guess why,
Beneath his pause and stalling eye.
But every "huh?" and nervous breath,
Spoke volumes in that quiet death.

For sometimes truths don't need a shout
They whisper loudest through our doubt.

Ecclesiastes 12:14 (KJV)

"For God shall bring every work into judgment, with every secret thing, whether it be good, or whether it be evil."

"When the Score is Kept"

In heated tones, a list was read,
Of all the things you "should've" said.
Not in the moment, clear and plain
But it flung like arrows, laced with blame.

You stood there still, your mind confused,
Your efforts mocked, your trust abused.
For every deed, a fault was found
Too soft, too loud, too lost, too bound.

You did the thing they asked you to,
But still we're told it wouldn't do.
Too much, too little, wrong, or late
Their shifting rules would be arbitrated.

This tactic, though, is known by name
A power play within the game.
Control disguised as slight critique,
Where goalposts move from week to week.

What once was right is now undone,
Approval fades as soon as I win.
It's not your fault you feel this way
The rules keep changing every day.

And when the past is weaponized,
Stored wounds unleashed, not analyzed,
It speaks not truth, but just intent
To win the war, not mend what's bent.

If grievances had space to grow,
In therapy, they'd start to show.
But buried deep and thrown in strife,
They sharpen hurt and cut like knives.

A partner's role is not to reign
With endless judgment, guilt, or shame.
If wrong you are no matter what,
The bond itself begins to rot.

So, hear this now, your heart's not weak
You're not the villain that they speak.
Exhaustion grows when blame won't cease,
And love can't thrive without some peace.

Let arguments not be on the stage
For hidden scores and silent rage.
Let truth be told where it belongs
In calm, in care, not fights prolonged

1 Corinthians 13:5 (KJV)

"Charity doth not behave itself unseemly, seeketh not her own, is not easily provoked, thinketh no evil;"

"I Heard the Sorry"

I heard the sorry in the dark,
A quiet spark, a muted mark.
You thought I slept, but I was still,
And silence broke against my will.

You whispered soft, like truth half-dead,
But every word still burned and bled.
A single sound just one so small,
Yet loud enough to say it all.

Was it for lies you never told?
A secret touch that turned you cold?
A night you left with no excuse
A bond you bent, a vow you lost.

Was it the way you've pulled away,
While acting fine from day to day?
You think I miss the subtle drift
But I can feel the growing rift.

I've seen your guilt in sideways glances,
In too-long stares and second chances.
Your hugs feel hollow, lips delayed,
A love once loud now half decayed.

That "sorry" echoed more than sound,
It dug up truths beneath the ground.
It told me things you'd never say
The ghost of what you gave away.

You said it thinking I would sleep,
But secrets never slumber deep.
I felt the crack beneath your voice,
Regret that shivered through your choice.

So now I ask don't dodge, don't lie
What truth made you afraid to try?
I'm not a fool, I've read the air,

There's something wrong, and you put it there.

Still, here I am, heart open wide,
But aching from what you can't confide.
Don't let your "sorry" be the end
Say what you meant, or don't pretend.

Luke 8:17 (KJV)

"For nothing is secret, that shall not be made manifest; neither anything hid, that shall not be known and come abroad."

"When Truth Rhymes Louder Than Lies"

I penned some lines, not sharp, but true,
And post them where light breaks through.
No names, no blame, just words with weight,
Still, you called me quickly, irate.

The ink was barely set to dry,
When fear lit fire behind your eye.
You felt exposed, like truth had caught
The parts of you thought I'd not.

Defensiveness that sudden roar
Came not from peace, but something more.
A nerve was struck, a mirror held,
You feared the truths my pen compelled.

I posted love your family, grace
But timing told a different case.
From silence, now a sudden show,
When love is real, it doesn't crow.

You brought me gifts, then pulled away,
The sun turned into a storm by end of day.
A token here, but talk? You fled
And left my questions cold in bed.

School forms brought blankness to your face,
As if your mind had left the place.
Your body home, your spirit gone,
A quiet war you carried on.

At 4 a.m., a hidden shower,
The scent of shame, not soap or power.
The bottles buried, secrets sealed,
But in the trash, the truth was revealed.
"Nice underwear," you said, detached
Like love was something you mismatched.
You didn't see the soul beneath,
Just skin to mask the guilt you sheath.

You touch with hands but not with heart,

You kiss but keep your depths apart.
Your love comes dressed in camouflage,
Not presence, just a sweet mirage.

This isn't trauma raw and healing,
Its pattern is masked by charm and reeling.
To give just enough, then pull away
A dance of shadows in the day.

But I was open, bare, and whole,
I brought my truth, my heart, my soul.
You couldn't meet me where I stood,
Not because you couldn't but never would.

I asked for things I have the right
To feel secure, to sleep at night.
To know the love I give is real,
And not some cage you only feel.

Your anger proved the poem true,
It wasn't me the mirror was you.
If words unmask what you conceal,
Then maybe it's not art you feel.

My spirit sensed before the proof,
The silence cracking under truth.
Your storm had started long before
My poem reached the public door.

And no, I'm not "too much," or blind,
I see with soul, I trust my mind.
I didn't write to wound or fight
I wrote because it wasn't right.

This wasn't despite being inside.
A pattern traced in prose and light.
A testament, not cry for war
To say, "I see you. I want more."

But now I see what's there, unmasked,

A man who flees when he is asked
To step into the heat of truth,
To love beyond the charm of youth.

You felt exposed. You feared the fall.
You knew I saw behind it all.
And still I stand, calm and aware
I am not crazy I was there.

Psalm 64:2-6 (KJV)

"Hide me from the secret counsel of the wicked;
from the insurrection of the workers of iniquity:
Who whet their tongue like a sword,
and bend their bows to shoot their arrows, even bitter words:
That they may shoot in secret at the perfect: suddenly do they shoot at him, and fear
not.
They encourage themselves in an evil matter:
they commune of laying snares privily;
they say, Who shall see them?"

"I When the Weather Changed"

The day began with golden light,
The kids and I were in pure delight.
We chased the sun, we shared some laughs,
On winding walks and garden paths.

An ice cream truck, a cheerful sound,
Our feet are like feathers on the ground.
I taught her balance, watched her try,
As hope lit stars inside her sky.

Then home you came, all cool and kind,
With treats and tools in mind.
You smiled, you played the thoughtful part
But something chilled beneath your heart.

I spoke of joy, the simple wins,
Of dusty shoes and sticky chins.
Of how our girl rode just today
You looked, then turned your gaze away.

I mentioned school and forms once more,
You drifted off, your eyes unsure.
The silence heavy, hard to bear,
Like I was speaking to thin air.

So off I walked with our small boy,
His laughter still my place of joy.
A quiet stroll, a calm escape,
While you and distance both took shape.

I swept the floor, then mopped it clean,
Like scrubbing off what could've been.
Then bathed our son with tender grace,
Still searching for your missing face.

You cooked, then said you'd take a shower,
Then come to bed in a late hour.
But not to hold or share my breath
You asked to lie on me like death.
A joke? A line? It made no sense.

It felt so cold, so far from hence.
Then "good job" said to underwear
A compliment? Or vacant stare?

And come dawn, I saw the proof,
Two bottles hidden under roof.
The steam still fresh, the night has gone stale
What story hides behind this veil?

What weight is drowning out your voice?
What pain has stolen all your choice?
Are you afraid, ashamed, or numb?
Why drink alone until you're dumb?

This house was joy before you came,
Now I feel small, confused, to blame.
You bring your clouds, not rain from skies
But storms that hide behind your eyes.

You smile, then shift, then disappear,
Your love runs cold when I draw near.
You say you'll come when I'm asleep
Why only then? What truths do you keep?

Your silence shouts, it fills the air,
Your distance leaves me stripped and bare.
I gave you space, I gave you light,
But you retreat into the night.

And yet, I know what I have felt,
My soul recoiled, my spirit knelt.
Not fear, but sorrow told me loud
This love is drowning in a cloud.

I'm not too soft, I'm not naïve,
My heart just longs for air to breathe.
A strong partner, who hears my truth
Not ghosts who vanish in their youth.

So, hear me now I will protect

My peace, my joy, my self-respect.
I will tune in, I won't dismiss
The aching absence in your kiss.

If there's a battle you won't name,
Don't drag me through your silent flame.
You owe me more than veiled goodbyes,
Then "good jobs" flung at covered thighs.

I see the signs. I feel the weight.
This isn't love. This isn't fate.
This is a call a bell, a scream
To wake me from this muted dream.

I wanted love. I gave you grace.
But now I crave a safer place.
If you can't meet me heart to heart,
Then let me go, don't play the part.

I deserve laughter without fear,
A touch that's kind, a voice sincere.
Not walking eggshells through your storm
But warmth that heals, a love that's warm.

The weather changed when you came in
But I won't drown beneath your wind.
I'll build a roof; I'll plant a tree.
And keep my sunlight here with me.

Isaiah 32:17-18 (KJV)
*"And the work of righteousness shall be peace;
and the effect of righteousness quietness and assurance for ever.
And my people shall dwell in a peaceable habitation,
and in sure dwellings, and in quiet resting places."*

"Sacred Strength"

What I've lived through is more than pain,
It's etched in layers, like weathered grain.
A quiet echo through my soul,
The truth is too vast to just console.

There were words that sounded sweet and sure
"I love you, trust me, we'll endure."
But words alone soon lost weight,
When actions failed to validate.

I stood alone while life moved on,
Through illness, fear, with strength drawn long.
No steady hands, no anchored ground,
Just empty air where cares not found.

Each small neglect, a subtle cue,
Spoke louder than the words I knew.
Not about the cost or pay,
But what was missing day by day.

I needed more than passing care,
I needed love that would be there.
A presence firm, a steady light,
No absence veiled on a quiet night.

And when I raised the truth I saw,
The silence deepened, cold and raw.
I questioned what was wrong or right,
While shadows blurred my inner light.

My needs were voiced, yet pushed aside,
My soul dimmed down, my heart denied.
But now I rise, I find my say,
And redefine what I'll let stay.

If "you're my world" lacks living proof,
Then I must ask, "Where is the truth?
For love that's real will share the load,
Not leave me lost on that same road.

A path one sided, worn and bare,
Where promises just weren't there.
And if no change comes when I speak,
Then love was never meant to keep.

Somewhere in me the lines grew thin,
My voice grew quiet, deep within.
I dimmed my light to make things whole,
But still, God whispered to my soul

"You are gold, not meant to bend,
This is not where your story ends."
The words I write through storm and flame
Are not just pain they stake my claim.

A ring, a name, without respect
That isn't love. That's just neglect.
And now I choose the clearer view
Peace over dreams that won't come true.

So now I ask with open eyes,
What if I loved me just as wise?
What if the care I freely gave
Was mine to keep, my soul to save?

Maybe silence. Maybe space.
A sacred pause to find my place.
But one bold move, one soul decree,
Will tell the stars I now choose me.

This book I write, not just with ink,
Is how I rise, is how I think.
There's no defeat inside my name
This is my power, lit by flame.

I survived. I wrote. I rose above.
That's not just pain. That's sacred love.
Let them witness what I ignite
I am the storm. I am the light.

Isaiah 40:31 (KJV)

"But they that wait upon the Lord shall renew their strength;
they shall mount up with wings as eagles;
they shall run, and not be weary;
and they shall walk, and not faint."

"The Mirror of Truth"

Your mother wears a shield,
Of guilt and shame not yet revealed.
She calls me "weak," she says I fear,
But it's her past that whispers near.

She left him once her silent ache,
Now paints him perfect, no mistake.
To call him out would crack her frame,
Expose her role, re spark her shame.

So, when he acts with sly deceit,
And I confront him firm, not sweet
She steps in swift, begins her play,
And shifts the blame my loving way.

She calls me "jealous," says I'm blind,
Yet it's her guilt that clouds her mind.
Her voice defends, her eyes deflect,
She needs his flaws to stay unchecked.

For if he's wrong, then she must see,
That motherhood fell short, maybe.
But I will not absorb her pain,
Or let her gaslight me again.

He talks to women late at night,
Their photos flashing in the light.
The chats are secret, laced with lust,
Yet I'm accused of lacking trust.
It's not my fear, it's his offense
This isn't love; it's no pretense.
When I feel hurt, it's not a test,
It's truth that rises in my chest.

Boundaries break, my voice ignored,
He guards his phone, not our accord.
His mother cheers, she plays her role
An ally tearing at my soul.

Your feelings, dear, are carved in gold.
Your strength is silence, calm, and bold.
His mother claims your love's a threat,
But what she fears is her regret.

You are not his shield or shrine,
Not built to fix what's not divine.
A partner walks with you in light,
Not hiding in shadows every night.

This is a dance of karmic threads,
Of wounds unhealed, and words unsaid.
But don't absorb what isn't yours,
Close spiritual, emotional doors.

Your role is not to hold their storm,
But to stay whole, and soft, and warm.
Discern the truth, align with grace,
Protect your peace, reclaim your space.

A mother's guilt should not define
What's healthy, good, or truly kind.
A partner's love should never ask
That you stay silent, wear a mask.

A coach would look and clearly see
This lacks respect and empathy.
Your boundaries broken, night by night,
That's not love its loss in flight.

Is this the path you've walked for years?
Through silenced cries and hidden tears?
Or will you rise and claim your say,
And walk if needed far away?

Isaiah 5:20 (KJV)

*"Woe unto them that call evil good, and good evil;
that put darkness for light, and light for darkness;
that put bitter for sweet, and sweet for bitter!*

"The Comment That Bent the Light"

I stood in my joy, in a radiant flow,
Where spirit and self-love began to grow.
Hair like a halo, heart full and wide,
Grace in my steps, and peace as my guide.

Then came a remark, tossed into the air,
"I'm surprised your knees can still do that there."
Laughter disguised it, a joke he might say
But shadows can travel in words that play.

A smile on my lips, but a flicker inside,
A ripple of doubt that I couldn't quite hide.
For under the joke lay a subtle refrain,
Of age, of appearance, of bodily strain.

It wasn't cruel but it caught me off beat,
A stone in my shoe while I danced in the street.
From affirmed to confused in the blink of an eye,
It felt like his words made my spirit run dry.

Could he not see how my soul was aligned?
Or was he just lost in a different mind?
His tone didn't mirror the light that I gave,
Instead, it was passive, uncertain, half brave.

So, I answered in metaphor, veiled and discreet,
With a tale from a show, not a word of defeat.
I painted my pain in a character's scene,
Because truth can be sharp when it's spoken to clean.

I didn't confront, was the safety not there?
Was I reading a silence that hung in the air?
Did I sense his defenses, his fragile disguise,
That shrinks from reflection or guilt in the eyes.

Emotionally mismatched, we danced out of tune,
He spoke out of dusk while I basked in the moon.
And though I had shimmered, aglow and secure,
His words were a crack that I tried to endure.

Spiritually speaking, the day had been bright,
Till his comment bent sideways the stream of my light.
Yet maybe this moment, though painful and stark,
Was showing me shadows I'd missed in the dark.

It tested my roots, asked, "Are you still whole
When someone else shakes the peace in your soul?"
And though he fell silent retreating, unclear
I held to my truth as my vision grew near.

His silence, perhaps, was confusion or shame,
Or a fear to be cast in a less gentle name.
Maybe my metaphor hit where it hurt
A mirror reflecting emotional dirt.

But I moved with grace, with indirect might,
Naming the wound without starting a fight.
It's artful, symbolic, a deep healing craft,
To soften the truth in a lyrical draft.
And though he said little, the silence was loud
A pause full of meaning that hung like a cloud.
I'll honor my beauty, my rhythm, my fire,
Not let one offhand line pull me out of the choir.

So, here's to the moments that test what we feel,
That asks if our joy and our power are real.
To holding the light when another goes dim
Still singing, still dancing, still trusting in him.

But more than in him, I trust now in me,
In my truth, my intuition, my need to be free.
Not from love but from self-doubt and sway
I rise, knees strong, dancing anyway.

Proverbs 18:21 (KJV)

"Death and life are in the power of the tongue: and they that love it shall eat the fruit thereof."

"When Eyes Wake Late"

How do you live like this
Where love feels more like hit or miss?
Where silence lingers, cold and wide,
Till someone else stands by your side.

You ask, "What should I do, how act?"
The truth is buried in the facts
He sees your glow when others praise,
But not in your unspoken days.

He's grown so used to all you give,
He's lost the thrill of watching you live.
Only when rivals raise their voice,
He acts as though you were his choice.

But love that wakes me from fear and doubt
It is not the kind to care about.
It's not your worth that changed or grew
It's just his pride that's fearing you.

Some only see when they might lose,
When you're admired by someone new.
And then, they beg with jealous eyes,
But love should never wear disguise.

Protect your heart its sacred space,
Don't chase a hand that won't embrace.
Stay grounded, strong in who you are,
You've always been your guiding star.

Ask not, "Will he fulfill my needs?"
But "Will I water my own seeds?"
Will you withdraw? Perhaps you must,
To find again your self-trust.

Limit the warmth you used to pour,
Till your own cup is brimming more.
Create the space your soul requires,

Fuel your goals, relight your fires.

Don't feel guilty for being seen
Let praise remind you what you mean.
Let joy and beauty lift your name,
And show you what's become too tame.

You are not worthy now
You've always held a sacred vow
To grow, to shine, to live with grace
Not begging for scraps in your own place.

So, if he sees you only when
Another voice says look again,
Then hold your power, claim your song
You've known your value all along.

Proverbs 4:23 (KJV)

*"Keep thy heart with all diligence;
for out of it are the issues of life."*

"The Pause Between the Lines"

He asked, "Just hold, I've got a call,"
You nodded, knowing work meant all.
You gave him space, you let him be,
Respecting time and boundaries free.

But when he came back, something changed,
Your voice, though calm, was slightly strained.
You asked, "That call what was it for?"
But laced with tone that questioned more.

He blinked, then paused, said, "Huh?" again,
His voice was soft, unlike back then.
A fidget here, a glance away,
His calm had seemed to slip astray.

The words came slow, like pulled from mist,
As if the truth had met a twist.
A guilty twitch, a nervous laugh,
As though he walked a shadowed path.

Was it the tone that made him freeze?
Or secrets blowing in the breeze?
A lie perhaps he tried to build,
While silence in the room was filled.

He might have felt caught in a snare,
The weight of judgment in the air.
Or maybe truth just wouldn't flow,
Unsure of how much you should know.

So now you're left to guess why,
Beneath his pause and stalling eye.
But every "huh?" and nervous breath,
Spoke volumes in that quiet death.

For sometimes truths don't need a shout
They whisper loudest through our doubt.

Luke 8:17 (KJV)

*"For nothing is secret, that shall not be made manifest;
neither anything hid, that shall not be known and come abroad."*

"Whispers in the Quiet"

I feel your drift, a distant tide,
No anchor now, though once we'd glide.
You lock your phone, avoid my gaze,
Your love once warm now hides in haze.

You smile less deeply, your eyes look far,
Like chasing shadows, chasing stars.
You're home but lost, your touch is cold,
Your stories are shaky, half retold.

You dress with care for nights unknown,
But not for me, you're not alone.
Excuses bloom like weeds at night,
While truth retreats from morning light.

You whisper late, then claim it's work,
But in your tone, the secrets lurk.
You dodge my love, then spark with blame,
As if my doubts should bear the shame.

The scent you wear was not for me,
It rides the wind too recklessly.
A shirt misplaced, a stranger's name
Too many signs to play this game.

Your kisses fade like evening light,
You chase the dark, avoid the bright.
And though you swear there's no one new,
My soul knows lies too well from truth.

Yet still I wait, beneath the ache,
To see if love was ever fake.
But silence speaks what lips conceal
What once was ours, someone else may feel.

So, tell me now, or let it be,
For love can't live in secrecy.
I'd rather hurt with truth laid bare,
Then sleep beside a vacant stare.

Proverbs 27:6 (KJV)

"Faithful are the wounds of a friend; but the kisses of an enemy are deceitful."

"A Truth Unfolds in Rhyme"

You read my poem, felt the burn,
The truth is too bright, too hard to turn.
You texted quick, a sweet "Hey babe?"
A tether tossed, control to save.

Not love, not care, but just a thread,
To stitch control through what I said.
You saw your image start to crack
So, you reposted, pulling back.

You praised your part, you played it proud,
A "partner" poses to please the crowd.
But where were you when I bled ink,
When I laid down what I feel and think?

My verses weren't a petty sting,
They named the ghost beneath the wing.
Unmet needs and blurred up lines,
A heart that cried through warning signs.

No "like," no love, you looked away,
Yet tried to show we're still okay.
Your silence loud, your signal mixed
Emotion dodged, connection fixed.

You fear my strength, my voice, my stance,
You flinch when I outgrow the dance.
I set a line; I drew it clearly
And that became your deepest fear.

Avoidance wears a quiet face,
It pulls back love and leaves no trace.
But still, you act the noble role,
A co parent with a sainted soul.

Yet underneath, there lies a game,
Where "good guy" masks the guilt and shame.
You'd rather charm than dive deep,

You barter peace, but truths don't sleep.

This poem was my sacred flame,
A cry for change, not praise or blame.
I spoke the truth I long denied
You flinched, deflected, ran to hide.

You post and praise to shift the light,
To dodge the heat, avoid the fight.
But I'm no longer holding back,
No softer tones, no painted track.

I voiced my need, I claimed my space,
And watched you scramble to save face.
But love that's real can take the fall,
And still show up when truth stands tall.

So, here's the line, the parting bell
I'll no longer shrink myself to "well."
The cost of peace is far too steep,
If I must silence what runs deep.

You had a chance to hear my soul,
Instead, you tried to take control.
But now the mask begins to slip
The truth is free, and I won't go on a trip.

I walk ahead with clearer skies,
No longer dimming for disguise.
This is my light, this is my stand,
No mixed-up love, no sleight of hand.

John 8:32 (KJV)

"And ye shall know the truth, and the truth shall make you free."

"The Guessing Game"

You walked slowly, your silence loud,
Your furrowed brow a thundercloud.
I made my breakfast, nothing grand
But something shifted in your stance.

You brought a gift without a word,
And in my bowl, offense was heard.
No voice, just looks that made me crawl,
As if my breakfast broke it all.

Your eyes, they darted, was it pain?
Or was it just a subtle game?
You scratched your head like I'd done wrong,
Though I had waited all day long.

No time was set, no plan made clear,
Yet when you came, I felt fear.
The film began, the lights went low,
But not a soul had let me know.

You acted kind, then turned away,
With silent storms you wouldn't say.
Each look, each sigh, a coded cue
A test I never even knew.

So now I ask what's real?
Why must I guess how you feel?
Why must I chase your shifting tone,
While never feeling quite at home?

Is this a gift, or is it debt?
Am I a partner or a pet?
Do acts of care have strings so tight
They bind my freedom out of sight.

You say your care, but never speak,
Then flinch when I seem strong, not weak.

The rules are yours, but never told
Control, disguised in cold gestures.

I shouldn't have to read your mind,
To dance on eggshells all the time.
You say so much without a sound,
Your silence shakes the solid ground.

I feel unsafe, though hands don't bruise
Just in the ways you make me lose.
My peace, my truth, my steady flame,
All flicker in this guessing game.

If kindness comes with quiet score,
That's not a gift, it's something more.
Its pressure wrapped in sweet disguise,
A love that watches, then denies.

I want a love where I can breathe,
Not walking on glass or subtly grieving.
A place where "no" is still okay,
And joy is not a game we play.

So, if you care, then speak it loudly
Don't make me read the shifting cloud.
For love should feel like steady rain,
Not weather built to cause me pain.

You may not shout, you may not scream,
But even quietly breaks the dream.
And when I say, "I feel unsafe,"
That's not a fear it's truth and grace.

Because real love is not a test.
It's not a puzzle or a guess.
It's voice and choice and honest light,
It's showing up and being right.

So, hear me now, or let me go,
For I won't shrink to make love grow.

I won't decode your quiet storm
I need a love that keeps me warm.

1 Corinthians 14:33 (KJV)

"For God is not the author of confusion, but of peace, as in all churches of the saints."

"The Architecture of My Knowing"

You cried on the phone,
said it was about something else.
But the story trembled
a thread pulled loose from a quiet lie.
"The call was short," you said,
vague as fog,
and I, clear as morning,
felt the ache behind the curtain.

Face in hands,
grief in bed
but was it grief for them
or for something you couldn't name?

I'd shared my plan for the morning,
I prepared what I could,
but you arrived at night,
not to support,
to rewrite.
That's not care.
That's control in disguise.

You preempt my effort
then call it love.
But your service is currency,
moral credit earned
to muffle your shame.

You moved instead of speaking.
You worked instead of resting.
You cried instead of sharing.
You acted instead of asking.

I see you
polishing surfaces
as if clarity lives in shine.
Wiping away what you won't confess.
This isn't intimacy.

It's management.

And I, in the middle of night,
watched you rearrange
my peace
into a performance.
You say it's collaboration,
but it feels like erasure.

My intuition isn't insecure.
It's a siren in my spine
a whisper I won't override.
This is perception,
not paranoia.

Are you here to meet me,
or just to handle me?

You cry,
but won't clarify.
You tidy,
but don't connect.
You say, "I love you,"
but skip the hard truth.

It's the pattern that stings
you undo what I've done
not to help,
but to hold control.
And in all of this,
I feel like a project,
not a partner.

You explain
instead of exploring.
You justify
instead of reflecting.
You apologies,
but orbit around intent,
never touching impact.

Yes,

you're showing guilt
but guilt isn't close
Shame is not a substitute
for presence.

I offered the morning.
You brought the midnight.
I offered plans.
You brought performance.

When I say "No,"
I'm not closing a door
I'm honoring my knowing.

My body is my oracle.
My gut, a compass of fire.
And it says:
This doesn't feel safe.
This doesn't feel sacred.
This doesn't feel like home.

You say,
"I've been 100% honest."
But absolutes are armor,
not truth.
You're not lying
you're protecting
A version of yourself
you think I can love.

You don't ask how I felt.
You just explain why you did it.
That's not listening.
That's strategy.

You say you see my effort
You just wanted to help.
But help born of guilt
is help that harms.
You don't honor the plan

you overwrite it
with your shame.

You said,
"It wasn't a pattern I recognized."
And that is the pattern.

I am doing emotional algebra.
I am solving for X,
where X is your unspoken grief.
I am an architect
of understanding the structure
of our disconnect.

You are just now seeing
what I've been holding alone.

You say,
"Let me in."
But I want you to stand still
to stop trying to fix
what you refuse to name.

I'm not asking for tears.
I'm asking for truth.
Not urgency
honesty.
No apology
accountability.

I don't feel safe.
I don't feel seen.
I don't feel chosen
in the daylight.

You come alive at 1:43am,
but love does not live
only in midnight effort.

This is not punishment.
This is perception.
This is the breath before boundary.

I deserve a partner who says:
"I see how that landed.
I acted from guilt, not grace."
Someone who stands beside me
when the lights are on
not just when shame
demands a spotlight.

This is not overthinking.
This is sacred noticing.
This is the wisdom
in my spine, chest, and breath.

I am not waiting anymore
for the version of you
that only appears
under fluorescent light
and regret.

I want more than performance.
I want partnership.

I'm not walking away from love.
I am walking toward truth.

And if that means walking alone
So be it.
My peace is worth the space.

Proverbs 4:7 (KJV)

"Wisdom is the principal thing; therefore get wisdom: and with all thy getting get understanding."

"1:43 A.M. The Words You Said"

You stayed downstairs the whole long day,
Avoiding light, then slipped away.
Not like you this silent game,
As if your soul won't speak my name.

At 1:43 you came to bed,
No words before, no tears you shed.
No reason clear, no work, no play,
Just stay apart and keep away.

You whispered low, "I love you," late
But love like that, it doesn't wait.
It doesn't hide behind the night,
It holds you close in morning light.

I felt the weight beneath your voice,
Not tenderness, but a hollow choice.
Were you feeling guilt or shame?
You spoke the words, but not the flame.

Was someone else on the other line?
Did secrets steal what once was mine?
You pull away, then come in near
When silence makes the coast feel clear.

You're not a night owl; I know your ways.
You don't just drift for empty days.
This wasn't rest or tired mind
It smelled of truth you left behind.

And every time you disappear,
Then speak as if your love is clear,
I wonder if you feel at peace
Or just afraid the cracks will crease.

"I love you" lands like a gentle lie
When followed by no how or why.
When distance ruled the day we spent,

But not one word to where you went.

You didn't speak of what was torn,
You just returned like nothing's worn.
But hearts don't mend in shadowed speech
I need the truth, not arms that reach.

You skip the part where pain is named,
Where space is held, where trust is claimed.
You come when I am half asleep,
When wounds are soft and guards don't keep.

I'm hurt, I'm raw, I'm left to guess,
While you retreat into your mess.
And though I try to stand and stay,
You love in bursts, then drift away.

This isn't how connection grows,
It isn't care if no one knows
What lies beneath the quiet door,
Where presence used to mean much more.

Your love feels timed, like it appears
To hush my doubts and mask my fears.
But silence doesn't heal the ache,
And whispered words can still be fake.

I'm not a mind to solve or chase,
I'm not a body taking space.
I'm someone real with needs unmet,
A soul that's starting to forget.

Forget how love once felt alive,
How it would reach and not just dive
Into the bed at night to say
What could've been said all the day.

And maybe, yes, you're hurting too,
And "I love you" was the best you knew
But love, when real, does not delay
Or only show at end of day.
You say the words, but not the why

And I'm left here to question, cry.
My body flinched, it did not glow
It told me things I didn't know.

And deep inside, I feel the scale
Of giving more and watching fail.
Of feeding love from empty hands,
While waiting for you to understand.

So, this, my love, was not just late,
Not just a phrase to compensate.
It was a mirror held to light
That showed me something isn't right.

I won't eat crumbs and call it care,
I won't pretend love is there.
If you can't show up through the day,
Then words at night won't make me stay.

I need the kind that meets my eyes,
That speaks in truth, not in disguise.
A love that shows, not one that hides
That holds my hand, not just my side.

So, hear me now, and hear me clearly:
"I love you" can't erase the fear.
If we are real, then let's begin
But not at night. And not like this again.

1 John 3:18 (KJV)

"My little children, let us not love in word, neither in tongue; but in deed and in truth."

"They Felt My Silence Speak"

I wrote in ink what broke in me,
A wound disguised in poetry.
No names were carved, yet somehow, still
It stirred the ones who felt the chill.

I bled my truth through quiet art,
While they kept secrets in the dark.
A thousand eyes, a hundred lies,
And friends who watched but never tried.

Now silence grows where trust once lived,
Their guilt is too loud to just forgive.
They scatter fast, avoid my gaze,
Afraid of all my soul conveys.

One message comes, so out of place,
A smile that cannot mask disgrace.
Weeks of quiet, now this note
Not love its fear in what she wrote.

She thinks I don't, but yes, I know.
My heart screamed months before the show.
The timing? Off. The words? A mask.
A subtle probe in friendship's cask.

They wonder if I've pieced it through,
If poems told them what I knew.
But truth, when whispered, still ignites
The parts of them hide from light.

A partner's kiss that wasn't mine,
A friend who crossed that sacred line.
And others watched, then turned their face
Now all their warmth has been replaced.

But I won't beg or chase a thread,
When love was fake, and trust is dead.
This isn't grief for just one lie

It's mourning bonds I can't revive.

They see my light and shield their eyes,
Because it burns through their disguise.
But I see clear I always did.
The truth was patient while they hid.

So let them run, deny, pretend
Their silence only helps me mend.
For those who vanish when I speak
We're never mine, they were just weak.

I walk alone, but not in lack,
I've got my soul, and it's intact.
This path is wide, this peace is deep,
And now I finally started to sleep.

Psalm 34:18

"The LORD is nigh unto them that are of a broken heart; and seventh such as be of a contrite spirit."

"No More Emotional Crumbs"

I gave my heart with open hands,
But you walked out with shifting sands.
On Father's Day, when love should stay,
You chose to vanish, drift away.

You blamed your job, a vague excuse,
Another thread in your old ruse.
A story told but left half stitched,
The truth, again, felt lost or switched.

This isn't just one fleeting night
It's patterns dancing out of sight.
Moments dodged and feelings missed,
A warmth replaced by cold, dismissed.

You come and go when it's most dear,
Around the times I hold most near.
You act as if we're still aligned,
But never pause to read my mind.

You never asked how I was torn,
Or what I felt that quiet morn.
You didn't check, you didn't see,
The ache that bloomed inside of me.

To love is more than being there
Its presence deep, its soul laid bare.
It's showing up with honest eyes,
Not feeding me with hollow lies.

I'm not confused, I'm not unsure,
I'm seeing things I can't ignore.
My spirit spoke, and now I trust
That self-love blooms in sacred dust.

You minimize, deflect, retreat,
Yet wonder why I feel defeated.
You want calm, avoid the storm,
But peace is born where truth is warm.

This isn't just about one day,
It's how you turn and slip away.
It's how you act like all is well,
While I'm left drowning in this shell.

I don't feel seen, I don't feel heard
Your silence is sharper than a word.
And every time you choose to escape,
It's one more wound I have to tape.

So now, I honor what I know
That love must water what it sows.
I won't keep begging just to be
A fleeting thought in your story.

I want a love that's wide and clear,
That shows up does not disappear.
Not one that leaves me in suspense,
Defending lies at my expense.

I will not plead for scraps again,
For half a heart or phantom friend.
I will not shrink, I will not bend
I'm not afraid to reach the end.

So, hear me now, and let it sting
You can't give less and call it king.
I'm not unkind, I'm not confused
I'm just done feeling so misused.

This is my truth, this is my stand
No more soft hurt swept by your hand.
No more pretending love still hums
I will not live on emotional crumbs.

Matthew 7:6 (KJV)

"Give not that which is holy unto the dogs, neither cast ye your pearls before swine, lest they trample them under their feet, and turn again and rend you."

"Don't Call Me Strong"

You pressed me down to lift your frame,
A fleeting act, but not a game.
You didn't ask, you didn't see,
The sacred space that is my body.

You laughed it off, "But you're so strong,"
As if that made your move less wrong.
You cloaked my pain in sweet disguise,
Deflected truth with hollow lies.

It wasn't rage, it wasn't hated
Just subtle weight that resonates.
But even small things leave a bruise
When dignity is what you lose.

You see, I've carried weight for years,
Absorbing doubt, dismissing tears.
My strength is not your right to test,
I set a line you crossed the rest.

That moment jarred my nervous core,
My cells recalled what came before.
The times I smiled, said I was "fine,"
While shrinking inward, toeing the line.

A temple touched without consent,
A sacred trust that came and went.
You pulled yourself, and I was there
But did you notice? Did you care?

Where was the pause to truly see,
The impact that you have had on me.
You could've asked, "Was that too much?"
But instead, you dulled the sting with crutch.

"Strong" is what you call me now,
To dodge the why, the when, the how.
You cloak discomfort, dodging the heat

But I won't make your wrong feel sweet.

This isn't wrath it's self-respect.
A plea for space you won't deflect.
I'm not your step, your leaning tree,
I'm sovereign and spirited myself.

Were you on autopilot flight?
Assuming that you had the right?
Believing strength means I won't break,
Or that I owe the hurt you make?

You touch, then vanish into mist,
In words and care, you don't persist.
No rhythm, no consistent grace
Just shifting tides, I can't embrace.

This is a reckoning, a line,
A call to own what you define.
To ask, to listen, not assume,
To clear the air, not fill the room.

You say you didn't mean to bruise
But at that moment, you still choose.
To guard your pride, not meet my eyes,
To feed me phrases, dressed as lies.

So, hear this truth, no sugar coat:
When you dismiss, you slit the throat
Of trust that tries to rise and bloom
You plant discomfort in its womb.

My strength is sacred, not your shield,
Not proof I'm fine, not sword I wield.
I'm not your reason to avoid,
The reckoning your hands deployed.

Next time, reach out with thought and care,
Not weight I didn't say I'd bear.
Respect is more than kind intent
It's how you act when words are spent.

For when you cross a line so slight,
And fail to make that crossing right
It's not just one small thing you do,
You tell me how you value you.

But I choose truth, and I choose me.
This voice, this body, soul, and plea.
No more erasure wrapped in praise,
No more dim light in gaslit haze.

So don't call me strong to make it right.
Own what you did. Step into light.
I'm not your lesson, not your song
I'm healing now. Don't call me strong.

1 Corinthians 6:19-20 (KJV)

*"What? know ye not that your body is the temple of the Holy Ghost which is in you,
which ye have of God, and ye are not your own?
For ye are bought with a price: therefore glorify God in your body, and in your spirit,
which are God's."*

"Mirror, Mirror, in the Yard"

I planted flowers with hands in pain,
While you sowed grass in the very same lane.
Not as support, not lending a hand
But to prove that you too could take a stand.

I was weary, aching, needing aid,
But your gaze was distant, your help was delayed.
Our child cried out, my breath ran low,
Yet you choose your tasks and let it go.

You mimic, mirror, match my pace,
Yet I miss the tears upon my face.
It isn't love when you compete,
While I collapse beneath my feet.

You saw me lead, so you took the wheel,
Not to care but to claim control you feel.
Your hands moved fast, your eyes stayed blind,
To the silent cries I left behind.

It's not support when you can't just be,
When every act must mirror me.
Your need to match is not the cure
It's driven by self-doubt, insecure.

You think, "She moves, then I must too,"
Not, "She's in pain what should I do?"
You watch me strain and then begin
To show your worth through tasks, not kin.

It's not enough to just appear,
While letting my world fall unclear.
I needed help, not imitation,
Not silence as your declaration.

You saw me limp, still held your line,
As if my hurt would be just fine.
You didn't reach, you didn't see

You thought, "Now it's time to focus on me."

This isn't love that meets in storm,
Its distance is dressed in mirrored form.
You didn't check, didn't ask, didn't stay
You just found something else to weigh.

Control does not care. It's not the same.
And matching tasks won't ease my flame.
You plant your grass while I near break,
Then I wonder why my voice might shake.

So, hear me now, in words that sting
Love is not a mirrored thing.
See me. Hold me. Break the mold.
Or lose the hand you failed to hold.

Galatians 6:2 (KJV)

"Bear ye one another's burdens and so fulfil the law of Christ."

"Daughter, You Are Not Alone"

You are of God, dear child, stand tall,
Though life may shake you, you won't fall.
For "greater is He that is in you," so true,
Then he that is in the world." (1 John 4:4 KJV), that strength is in
you.

You are not worthless, cast aside,
You're "fearfully made," you must not hide.
His "marvelous works" live deep in your soul,
(Psalm 139:14) you are valuable, beautiful, whole.

When voices scream lies, and hearts turn cold,
When love feels distant, and pain takes hold,
Look in the mirror, speak truth and grace,
You are a daughter of God no one can erase.

Abuse is not holy, not silence, not blows,
"The Lord executed righteousness," He knows.
(Psalm 103:6) He sees what they do in the dark,
You are His child His light, His spark.

"He delivered the poor in affliction," He'll stay,
(Job 36:15) opening your ears when you've lost your way.
Jesus once knelt by a woman condemned,
(John 8) He saw her pain; He chose to defend.

So, lift up your heart, even trembling and small,
Begin to pray through the ache of it all
"Lord, deliver me from this place of despair,
Help me hear Your truth louder than fear."

"A prudent man foresees the evil," and hides,
(Proverbs 22:3) God gives you discernment, not pride.
You are not called to suffer in vain,
There is wisdom in leaving emotional pain.

Start with a journal, a whisper, a plan,
Reach out to someone who will understand.

Not everyone sees, but God always will,
He gives courage to stand when the world grows still.

Speak truth but don't carry revenge in your hand,
For "vengeance is Mine," saith the Lord take your stand.
(Matthew 18:15) If he trespasses, let truth be your light,
Confront with calm, not with spite.

"The way you are treated is not God's design,
There must be peace for this heart of ours
For our child, for my soul, for the vows we made,
I will not let love be buried or fade."

"Keep thy heart with all diligence," protect it with care,
(Proverbs 4:23) don't let bitterness live there.
You're not just a partner, a mom, or a wife a
You're the keeper of peace, the gateway to life.

"If any provide not for his own," God is clear,
(1 Timothy 5:8) real love must draw near.
Your child deserves a home built on grace,
Not shadows and shouting and a hostile place.

"Two are better than one," so reach out your hand,
(Ecclesiastes 4:9–10) there is still a faithful band.
If your friends have vanished, find the ones who pray,
A church, a sister, who will help light your way.

"Wait on the Lord be of good courage," be still,
(Psalm 27:14) Let Him strengthen your will.
But don't wait in harm, that's not His request,
Jesus calls you to peace, to comfort, to rest.

"Come unto me, all ye that labor and are heavy laden,"
(Matthew 11:28) He gives rest to the soul so shaken.
He will never break a bruised reed in your hand,
He's the Rock you can trust, the One who understands.

So, hear this now, wherever you stand

You are not broken just battle scared.
You are not alone though the journeys are hard.
You are God's daughter beloved and known.
You are never forsaken, never on your own.

Step by step, He will show you the way,
One prayer at a time, one tear you don't say.
He walks with the weary, the wounded, the small,
He lifts the hurting He catches it all.

And when you're ready to rise from the pain,
He'll give you beauty for ashes, sunshine through rain.
Because you, sweet sister, are heaven's own art
A warrior in grace, with a lionheart.

You are not alone. God is with you and He is for you.
Hold on. Heal. Hope.
He will never fail you.

Isaiah 41:10 (KJV)

*"Fear thou not; for I am with thee: be not dismayed; for I am thy God:
I will strengthen thee; yea, I will help thee; yea, I will uphold thee with the right hand
of my righteousness."*

"The Pattern I Can't Unseen"

You haven't called.
Not a whisper. Not a word.
Only silence,
and the silence has learned to speak.

You said you "can't get on your page,"
but I've seen you vanish behind smaller things.
And this?
This feels like the kind of quiet that carries guilt
in its pockets like stones.

My poem was never just a poem.
It was a lantern dropped in a cave
you hoped I'd never find.

And then
You liked it.

Clicked "like" like you hadn't just read
your own reflection in the wreckage.
Clicked "like" like I couldn't possibly
be writing about you.

But what kind of man
like the poem that buries his name
beneath each trembling line?

What kind of truth
hides in plain sight,
smiling at the crowd?

Meanwhile,
she resurfaces
the friend who once held my laughter
now casually tapping "🖤" on my photos
like nothing's been dismantled.
What is that?
Guilt dressed in good manners.
A soft check-in to see if the storm is brewing.

She doesn't know I've already tasted the rain.

Is she soothing her conscience
or preparing for a reveal?
Does she think I don't see how
Your silences rhyme with hers?

Because I do.

You're not just separate ghosts.
You're echo in the same hallway.
One hides in distance,
The other hides in pixels.
Together,
you choreograph a silence too loud to ignore.

Maybe it wasn't physical.
Maybe it was words in the dark,
too many feelings in the wrong inbox,
a betrayal not of the body
but of the bond.

You say nothing happened,
but something always happens
before nothing starts.

Maybe you painted me harshly
to justify her closeness.
Maybe you liked how she listened
when you made it hard to love.

That, too,
is a kind of cheating.

And now,
with every gesture,
you manage suspicion like a PR campaign.

But guilt doesn't disappear.
It lingers.

In the call you don't make.
In the post she suddenly likes.
In the poem you tried to blend into.

You're not fooling me.
You're folding around me.
Avoiding the shape of the truth
because it doesn't fit
the version of you still wants me to believe in.

You didn't support me with that "like."
You didn't honor my pain.
You tried to sit beside it
without ever admitting
You were the reason I wrote it.

This isn't paranoia.
It's pattern.
And patterns don't lie
people do.

So, I'll stop asking questions
you pretend not to understand.

This poem is not a plea.
It's a door.

If this is the truth,
let it enter.
If this is the end,
Let it begin.

Because I deserve love
that doesn't live in shadows
or hide behind silence
or click "like"
when it should say:
"I'm sorry."

Psalm 55:12–14 (KJV)

*"For it was not an enemy that reproached me; then I could have borne it:
neither was it he that hated me that did magnify himself against me; then I would have
hid myself from him:
But it was thou, a man mine equal, my guide, and mine acquaintance."*

"Party Flirtation Turns into a Spectacle"

At a party glowing with laughter and wine,
You leaned in close like it wasn't a sign.
Your whisper slipped like a secret breeze,
And suddenly joy turned to uneasiness.

I saw your fingers brush his knee,
A spark too loud for just "friendly."
The room kept dancing, unaware
But my world cracked beneath the glare.

A photo snapped when no one knew,
The moment was framed in shameful hue.
It passed like gossip always does,
A hundred mouths, and none for us.

Your phone, I just borrowed a song,
It revealed a thread where hearts went wrong.
Flirty words and plans to meet,
Truth laid out in a private cheat.

A gasp. A glance. The story spread,
Behind my back, the whispers fed.
By the time the truth reached me,
It was old news for all but me.

At birthdays, concerts, crowded rooms,
I saw you drift like trailing fumes.
His hand on yours, your subtle s

Psalm 55:12–14 (KJV)

"For it was not an enemy that reproached me; then I could have borne it:
neither was it he that hated me that did magnify himself against me; then I would have
hid myself from him:
But it was thou, a man mine equal, my guide, and mine acquaintance."

"The Room Was Full, But I Was Alone"

In crowded rooms where laughter swirled,
You played your part, your charm unfurled.
A hand that lingered much too long,
A laugh too loud, a touch too strong.

I watched you lean, your whispers close,
The kind that only lovers know.
Your fingers brushed along a thigh,
And still, I stood I don't know why.

Among my friends my chosen few,
You sought out someone that I knew.
A face I trusted, arms once warm,
Now part of this unfolding harm.

Your gaze lit up when they walked nearby,
A playful smirk, clear intentions.
You shifted, changed when they were there,
More alive as if I wasn't there.

The room took note the glances passed,
A joke, a nudge, then silence cast.
I felt the weight of every stare,
While you pretended not to care.

A birthday toast, a engagement dance,
You gave that thief your second glance.
You danced with them, not just your feet,
But something sacred, in deceit.

Then came the texts I didn't seek,
But truth poured out from just one peek.
A friend who borrowed just your phone
Unveiled a thread that chilled the bone.

Photos sent and midnight chats,
Confessions dressed in cyber pats.
Your heart, it seemed, was on display,
But not for me you looked away.

And worse, the whispers weren't confined,
They reached the group, they intertwined.
The pity eyes, the sudden pause
As if I was the guilty cause.

The group chat changed the memes ran dry,
They tiptoed past while I walked by.
I was the last to learn it all,
The final punch before the fall.

You touched a match to what we built,
And scorched it deep in silent guilt.
Then dared to say I made it more
Too sensitive, as if unsure.

You turned my pain into a jest,
While wearing smiles, sharply dressed.
But every echo in that space,
I was laced with loss I can't replace.

So now I walk through once shared light,
Where every shadow knows my fight.
And though my voice may break and bend,
I know betrayal wears a friend.

The party's done. The truth remains.
A crown of thorns dressed up as flames.
You danced, you laughed when I stood, alone.
But now I rise. I make it known.

Psalm 41:9 (KJV)

"Yea, mine own familiar friend, in whom I trusted, which did eat of my bread, hath lifted up his heel against me."

"Emotional Cheating with a Friend"

You held their gaze when I looked away,
Shared laughs too long, too much to say.
Our secrets leaked through lips not mine
You found in them your place to shine.

You whispered pain I'd yet to hear,
To someone who once called me dear.
My flaws discussed in casual tone,
While I lay dreaming all alone.

You typed out hearts at midnight's door,
Flirted like we'd never swore.
Each message laced with heat or thrill
A quiet burn that time can't kill.

Not just the words, but how you stayed,
While boundaries bent, they broke, then swayed.
A friend became your second skin,
While I stood outside looking in.

One drunken night, or more than one,
A touch, a kiss beneath the sun.
A body shared where trust once stood,
Now buried deep beneath false good.

A smile, and charm,
Still close enough to do me harm.
Introduced by those I trust
And still, you dove. Betrayed. Unjust.

At parties, hands you'd intertwine,
In crowded rooms, you crossed the line.
A whisper here, a lingering glance,
A dance that wasn't just a dance.

My friend saw texts not meant to show,
Now all of them seem to know.
Their silence was loud, the room was cold,

A private wound turned public fold.

You laughed and said I'm "just intense,"
To friends you fed my confidence.
You made a move, they turned away
But still the damage chose to stay.

A past you never shared with me,
But shared with friends so carelessly.
I learned it last, in shameful hush,
Their sideways glances made me blush.

You made them promise not to speak,
Each lie a brick in walls that leak.
Their silence wasn't kind at all
It built a different kind of fall.

A love confessed you didn't end,
Another heart I called a friend.
And you, unsure, or worse enticed,
While loyalty was sacrificed.

Someone else got truth, not me,
The last to know what all could see.
Their guilt now sits where trust once bloomed
A garden lost, forever doomed.

You split the seams of bonds so tight,
By playing shadows into light.
You chose deceit as your refrain
And left me holding all the pain.

So, call it cheating, call it gray,
But hearts don't heal from shades that stay.
For what you touched was more than skin
You broke the sacred from within.

Psalm 41:9 (KJV)

"Yea, mine own familiar friend, in whom I trusted, which did eat of my bread, hath lifted up his heel against me."

"The Silence That Spoke"

You confided in my friends what I still don't know,
A storm in the shadows, a hidden low blow.
They carry a secret that bends every smile,
A guilt they've worn quietly now for a while.

You crossed a line in a place far too near,
Where trust turns to ash and truth disappears.
Messages whispered or touches too close
A moment with someone I trusted the most.

The room feels colder where laughter once stayed,
And eyes dart away like debts left unpaid.
Their silence is louder than words could convey,
A wall made of things they can't bear to say.

You spoke of our love like it meant far less,
Exaggerated my flaws in a casual mess.
You painted me crooked in stories you told,
And now their stares are distant and cold.

But the midnight "sorry" you softly exhaled,
Spoke volumes of truths you've carefully veiled.
It wasn't for fights or words misaligned
It echoed a secret still locked in your mind.

They hesitate now, unsure who to trust,
Split between justice, and old, broken lust.
The friendship I leaned on is splintered with doubt,
As if love's foundation is being pulled out.

There's something you've done that I've not been told,
A silence more chilling than nights left cold.
Perhaps they all saw, perhaps they all knew
And now they're protecting both me and you.

A fracture is forming, not loud but deep,
Where loyalty lingers and conscience won't sleep.
They're choosing their sides in a war not declared,
In glances, in distance, in pain shared and spared.

So here in this quiet, I'm left to unsee
A version of truth that won't come to me.
But I feel it like thunder before the rain,
The echo of heartbreak dressed up as shame.

If this is the end, then let it begin,
With honesty piercing the silence within.
For love cannot live where shadows reside
And truth is the only side I won't hide.

Psalm 41:9 (KJV)

"Yea, mine own familiar friend, in whom I trusted, which did eat of my bread, hath lifted up his heel against me."

"While I Slept"
(A Poem About Silent Guilt and Unspoken Words)

You whispered "sorry" in the dark,
While I was dreaming, still, and stark.
No light, no fight, no spoken scene,
Just soft shadows and in between.

You felt the weight you couldn't name,
A flicker caught inside your flame.
You did or said regret ran deep,
But I couldn't face me while I slept.

Afraid of how I might react,
You chose the quiet, pulled it back.
An echo buried in the night,
Avoiding truth, avoiding light.

You feared I'd turn, or break, or cry,
So let the moment pass you by.
Apology in whispered air,
As if asleep, I wouldn't care.

You stood beside me, love grown thin,
But guilt is too loud to keep within.
Yet still too scared to see it through
The cost of what I meant to you.

A passive hurt, a silent plea,
A coward's grace or honesty?
Instead of words with open eyes,
You masked your truth in lullabies.

Was it love? Or just regret?
A promise made you can't forget.
An inner war you can't confess,
Some secret still you won't address.

Perhaps you watched me, lost in thought,
And saw the peace you never brought.

And maybe then you tried to mend,
To start with the truth, you couldn't end.

But still, I ask what did you hide?
Was it a lie tucked deep inside?
A heart betrayed, a stolen trust,
A vow you shattered into dust.

Or was it pain you never voiced?
A haunted past, a wounded choice?
The kind of ache you never share,
So sorry it just hangs in the air.

You said your peace while I was gone,
While dreams kept moving slowly on.
You felt relieved, escaped the fight
But left me guessing in the night.

So here I lie, with nothing clear,
An echoed "sorry" in my ear.
And though you think you've done your part,
You never truly gave up your heart.

For next time, love, just speak to me
Not ghosts, not dreams, not quietly.
If what you feel is real and true,
Then say it loud when I see you.

James 5:16 (KJV)

"Confess your faults one to another, and pray one for another, that ye may be healed. The effectual fervent prayer of a righteous man availeth much."

"Honest Coffee"

You'd love that place, it's calm, refined,
Where brews are bold and truth's not blind.
The drinks are strong, no watered shame,
Not like some folks who dodge the blame.

Each sip is sharp, each pour is true,
Unlike the tales I'm fed by you.
No need for tricks or clever lines,
Real flavor doesn't hide behind signs.

You paced around, you played it slow,
Said "meeting," but it didn't show.
A photo sent, but late, rehearsed,
Truth never needs to be coerced.

A voice came through it rang too clear,
From someone you once held near.
Strange how the past begins to blend,
When present truths begin to bend.

I stayed composed, I smiled, I swayed,
But sugar masks the games you played.
You like your stories smooth and light,
I like my coffee brewed with bite.

We spoke of homes, of future days,
But some foundations fail to stay.
And while you danced through shifting air,
I sat in stillness fully aware.

So, drink your blend, rehearse your plot,
But know I saw. I knew. I caught.
And while you stirred your little doubt,
My silence steeped then poured it out.

Luke 8:17 KJV

"For nothing is secret, that shall not be made manifest; neither any thing hid, that shall not be known and come abroad."

In the quiet weight of all I've carried,
in the nights that felt endless and unseen,
it was God/Jesus who held me together
when I thought I would fall apart.

"God is our refuge and strength, a very present help in trouble." (Psalm 46:1, KJV)

Life does not move gently for any of us.
We all walk through valleys
through moments of pain, of doubt,
of feeling abandoned, betrayed, or overlooked.
There are days when loneliness echoes louder than hope.

"Yea, though I walk through the valley of the shadow of death, I will fear no evil: for thou art with me." (Psalm 23:4, KJV)

But even there especially there
you are not alone.

"I will never leave thee, nor forsake thee." (Hebrews 13:5, KJV)

Through every trial, every tear, every unanswered question,
God is with you.
He does not turn away.
He does not betray.
He does not leave.

"The Lord is nigh unto them that are of a broken heart." (Psalm 34:18, KJV)

Even when your heart feels empty,
even when your faith feels small,
His presence remains steady and unshaken.

"My grace is sufficient for thee: for my strength is made perfect in weakness." (2 Corinthians 12:9, KJV)

So, hold on.
Hold on when it's hard.
Hold on when it hurts.
Hold on when you don't understand.

"Be strong and of a good courage… for the Lord thy God is with thee whithersoever thou goest." (Joshua 1:9, KJV)

Because just as He carried me through,
He will carry you too.

"Casting all your care upon him; for he careth for you." (1 Peter 5:7, KJV)

Do not give up on God
because He will never give up on you.

"The Lord will perfect that which concerneth me." (Psalm 138:8, KJV)

www.ingramcontent.com/pod-product-compliance
Lightning Source LLC
Chambersburg PA
CBHW020841150726
48196CB00002B/160

9 798234 078315